Complete Horoscope 2019

Monthly astrological forecasts for every Zodiac sign for 2019

TATIANA BORSCH

ISBN: 9781729238523

Because of the dynamic nature of the Internet, any web addresses or links contained in
this book may have changed since publication and may no longer be valid. The views
expressed in this work are solely those of the author and do not necessarily reflect the
views of the publisher, and the publisher hereby disclaims any responsibility for them.

This book is a work of non-fiction. Unless otherwise noted, the author and the publisher
make no explicit guarantees as to the accuracy of the information contained in this book
and in some cases, names of people and places have been altered to protect their privacy.

Any people depicted in stock imagery provided by Getty Images are models,
and such images are being used for illustrative purposes only.
Certain stock imagery © Getty Images.

Lulu Publishing Services rev. date: 09/21/2018

CONTENTS

General Annual Forecast For Every Sign

ARIES

You keep moving forward. You have a great opportunity to reach the top, but the competition for the Grand Prize is going to be tough.

Job. Career. 2019 will bring you numerous opportunities to climb the ladder of professional success. But you must do a lot – never stop working on improving yourself, learn something new, and, of course, be a "Steadfast Tin Soldier." These are the necessary conditions for raising your career to a qualitatively new level.

Many representatives of your sign will have mutual interests with business partners from other cities or countries. On that road, they will come across both success and problems. The latter are most probable in January, March, June, and September. In these periods, you can face fraud, intrigues, inconsistent and sometimes hostile behavior of your foreign colleagues. In another variant, the international situation, new legislation and legal problems can hamper the collaboration.

The entrepreneurs and managers are advised to be more attentive to the documents, because inspections are quite probable in January, March, June, and September.

The good news is that all the problems of the coming year will turn out to be solvable. It will become clear in December, when you see that you made the right choice and spent time in the right way. Besides, you can start a business in another city or country.

Towards the end of the year, the employee can get a more prestigious and highly paid job. But before that, he/she should take care of his/her professional reputation and be more attentive to his/her colleagues.

Money. Your financial positions are stable, there is an obvious positive tendency. The largest amount will come in December, and it will be really a lot of money.

Love. Family. All kinds of things will be happening in your personal life. You will be very busy at work and have endless business trips. As a result, you will have too little time left to spend with your partner. This is why separation may begin, though quiet and almost unnoticed.

If this is the case and there are no other reasons making your relationship cooler, try to understand your partner's feelings, spend more time together, and, if necessary, explain your situation patiently.

However, if there are other reasons for the alienation and if it began a long time ago, it will be difficult to hold what is slipping out of hands. A new stage is underway in your life. You will meet with new people, which means that you will have to part with something and someone. This is an extreme case, of course, but there is a cause for concern. Try to find mutual understanding, avoid complaints and dramas. This won't be easy, but the sooner you understand it, the better it will be for everyone.

The singles will find themselves in a different situation: the new people they meet can become not only friends, but also their life companions for years to come.

Many representatives of your sign will plan to move to a new house/ apartment or to another city/ country.

Health. In 2019, you are active, energetic and quite healthy. But be careful throughout the year when traveling and driving.

TAURUS

A certain period of your life is coming to an end. 2019 manifests transition from the past to the future, which can be far from easy. Anyway, a new era is ahead, and there is no way back, you can only move forward.

Job. Career. In 2019, the professionally active representatives of your sign need to make a serious restructuring of their business. The entrepreneurs and managers will revise the goals of their business and make serious adjustments to it.

Many will have plans to expand their business, and, in some cases, this will involve another city or country. The old, time-tested ties will be very important. Your old friends as well as business partners living in faraway lands will do their best to support and help you.

The main problem of the coming year will be relations with some of your friends or high-position people. You can have ideological and financial disagreements, and, as the astrologer believes, you can hardly find a compromise. Negotiations can last throughout the year, some conditions will be met, but you will hardly agree on the main issues in 2019. Perhaps 2020 is better in this respect.

The stars recommend you not to trust promises and or rely on high-position individuals, no matter how reliable they may seem; otherwise, you will face difficulties and the result may be very sad.

For various reasons, the employee can quit his/her job and think about a different way of applying his/her talents. However, such opportunities will only appear in 2020, so before making the final decision to resign, remember that finding a new job can require a lot of time.

Money. Throughout the year, your financial positions are not stable, you will be spending money on a regular basis, either for business, or for personal life.

Many will have to pay off their debts and observe their past financial and other obligations.

In a word, you will have numerous expenses, while your revenues will decrease. Don't forget about it!

Love. Family. The wind of change will affect both romantic and family relationships. The loving spouses will start a big renovation or even buy a new home. In some cases, these labor-intensive events can take place far from home and require a lot of money.

In some families, relationships will change greatly. This mainly refers to those born in the period from April 21 to April 30: they will have revolutionary feeling and ideas and thus want to change their lives as well as family relations. It's hard to provide details, but there is definitely a cause for concern.

The parents will have large expenses related to their children. Many families may have new children or grandchildren.

For the lovers, this year is very difficult - separation may begin, though quiet and almost unnoticed. Don't try to hold what is slipping out of hands. A new stage is underway in your life, which means that you will have to part with something and someone.

Health. Throughout the year, your energy potential is not high, there is a chance of exacerbation of old diseases or unexpected appearance of new ones. Those who have hormonal system disorders or suffer diabetes should be especially cautious. They need a strict diet and constant medical follow-up.

Many representatives of your sign will have a tendency to gain weight, so do sports, eat healthy food, and exercise.

GEMINI

Different situations are possible in 2019. You may become very dependent on your business or romantic partners. Look for a compromise, although, sometimes, it won't be easy!

Job. Career. In terms of career, this can be a difficult year. You will have to prove to your entourage that you can work well under stress. The latter can be due to your business partners, who will be constantly changing their intentions and plans.

Perhaps they will try "to turn a solo", which, of course, will affect negatively both the relations and the business. There will also be many business-related issues, which looks very strange from the perspective of the stars. Your business lacks structure, has unclear goals and a very uncertain future. All the parties concerned should pay close attention to all that. Try to avoid direct confrontation and convince your partners that you need to work together. You can succeed in doing this in February, April, May, August, October, and December.

Confrontation is possible in March, June, July, and September. In these periods, there is a chance of conflicts related to different views on the development of the business as well as on finance, fighting for leadership, and other problems.

In the most difficult case, breakup is possible, while in the best-case scenario, there will reconciliation due to the desire to save the business. Both are quite likely in December. It will only be then that the confrontation comes to an end.

The employee will face serious competition. He/she is recommended to work diligently and, if possible, avoid conflicts with the boss, otherwise, problems will be unavoidable.

In another version, there will be changes inside the company, such as change of the boss, or absorption by a larger company. The lack of stability will make many of the employees look for alternative ways to apply their talents or think about starting their own businesses.

Money. In terms of finance, the year may be rather uneven, which is not surprising in this situation. However, there will be no bankruptcy as decent amounts of money will be hitting your account from time to time. This can be expected in late February as well as in March, May, July and, maybe, in November and December.

Love. Family. Big changes are underway in your personal life. The singles and those disappointed in their previous affections will have an important encounter, which will have a logical continuation - cohabitation or marriage.

At the same time, problems are possible related to the parents or senior family members, or to finding ways of living together.

The experienced spouses can count on the partner, whose business will improve significantly. However, problems are also likely here, such as alternative affections and hobbies, which always make life more difficult.

Towards the end of the year, there will be plans related to getting a new home, which will come true in 2020.

Health. In 2019, your energy potential is not high, the reasons being instability in business and love. No matter how busy you are, try to devote more time to yourself and remember the importance of walking, massage, sauna and spa. Don't forget that a 'healthy body equals a healthy mind'!

CANCER

This will be a busy though very uneven year. You will have to adapt to the constantly changing circumstances and work hard. However, the reward is worth it!

Job. Career. The good news of the coming year is that you won't be jobless no matter where you are. You will keep doing successfully the business started last spring, which will affect positively your finances – you will have much more money.

The employee's professional positions will also become stronger. Many will have to do their colleague's job in addition to their own, but, according to the stars, they will benefit from that greatly.

But, as it usually happens, luck will be accompanied by problems. Relations with some of the partners are far from ideal, there may be serious disagreements related to the development of the business or even dividing it. The battles can last throughout the year, and the most violent ones will happen in January, June, and July.

Those who have ties with partners from other cities or countries will also face difficulties. Colleagues from faraway will be changing their plans constantly, which will make the mutual business slow down or even stop. You will have to look for other options and partners, which you will definitely find towards the end of the year.

The entrepreneurs and managers of all levels should get ready for inspections, most likely in the first months of the year as well as in June and July. The auditors will stay at the company for a long time and cause a lot of problems.

Money. Your financial situation as a whole is stable, but various problems, both professional and personal, can cost you a pretty penny. Throughout the year, large expenditures will alternate with large incomes, but you will stay afloat anyway!

Love. Family. In 2019, your personal life will be rather complicated. The spouses who have been together for a long time will have permanent quarrels and often talk about divorce. In the most difficult cases, it will happen, but at the end of the year something will change again. Many will understand that "a bad peace is better than a good fight" and that the relationship is far from being over. You will see what exactly will happen in 2020, but there is a chance of reconciliation.

There is another option, namely, that the spouses who seemed inseparable will have to separate. But the situation will improve towards December - separated by time and distance, the couple will get together and be happy.

A similar situation is possible for the experienced lovers.

Health. Throughout the year, your energy potential is not high, so take care of yourself and lead an exceptionally healthy lifestyle. 2019 is ideal for doing sports as well as for quitting bad habits and finding good ones instead. Here is another piece of advice: throughout the year, be careful when traveling and driving.

LEO

In general, 2019 will be good for you. You will have a freedom of choice, many of your plans and dreams will come true. All you need to do is to be vivid, bold and fresh.

Job. Career. The second half of the year, especially its end, is the best time for your career. The entrepreneurs and managers will start a new project and spend most of the year on it. It won't be easy to get profit and become successful. The most significant in this regard are December 2019 and the whole of 2020. Before that time, you will have to do preparatory work and spend money, and the expenses can be much higher than planned. The stars recommend you not to overestimate yourself when starting an offensive.

The employee can get a new job or strengthen his/her position significantly at the current company. The late fall and winter of 2019 are also good for that.

Those who want to start their own business can do it in the coming year.

The year is good for the people of creative professions - their projects will be recognized, and their popularity will increase.

Money. In terms of finance, the year is not very good. You will have numerous and regular expenses related either to business or to personal life.

Love. Family. Numerous changes are underway inside your family. Your children are doing better, and your relations with them will improve. You can buy real estate as well as start a family business.

At the same time, the children may require a serious part of the family budget for education and growing up.

Many families may have new children or grandchildren.

Your relationship will bring you both joy and sorrow. The situation will be very uneven. In one case, the reason will be the different views on life and differing value systems, while in another, financial problems. But, despite the disagreements, there is a hope that, in the long run, love will triumph.

Health. Throughout the year, your energy potential is rather high and you will stay healthy.

It should also be noted that 2019 is very good for changing the image and the wardrobe, and even for plastic surgery, if the latter is required.

VIRGO

This year, you must put things in order both in business and in personal life and cover your bases in both.

Job. Career. In 2019, the entrepreneurs and managers will decide to expand their business and can buy real estate for that purpose. Taking care of the new premises as well as organizational work will last for almost the whole year, but definitely bring the goal closer. However, there will be problems on the way to success. One of them and, perhaps, the most important will be relations with some of the partners. People you counted on will behave in a rather evasive and contradictorily way, while in the worst-case scenario, they will resort to fraud. Conflicts will erupt throughout the year, and the situation may only normalize at the end of the year.

The good news will be strengthening of ties with the colleagues from other cities or countries. Those can be your old friends as well as loyal business partners. They will be your main support in the difficult times.

The employee can think of starting his/her own business or joining their family business.

The stars recommend those who keep working at their current company to be more attentive to their duties and avoid intrigue. They can easily lose their job in 2019, which should be borne in mind.

Money. In the coming year, your financial positions are rather unstable, the reason being numerous business- or family-related expenses.

Love. Family. For many representatives of your sign, the main events of this year will occur in your personal life. Many families will buy real estate for their own needs or for the needs of their grown-up children. For various reasons, relations with the adult children will be complicated. The latter experience a period of difficulties and need your attention, participation, and, of course, financial assistance.

Many families will have new children or grandchildren.

For the lovers, this year can be difficult. The relationships will be very unstable and, in some cases, will stop forever. The same goes for the quarrelling spouses. The stars recommend them not to ignore any misunderstandings, but discuss them sincerely. Nothing but complete clarity will help you avoid alienation, which is quite probable in the coming year.

Health. In 2019, your energy potential is not high, and the stars strongly recommend you to lead an exceptionally healthy lifestyle. These recommendations are relevant for all representatives of your sign and especially for those who have hormonal system problems as well as for people with diabetes. In 2019, you will tend to gain weight, so consider a healthy diet, walking and other useful health-improving procedures.

LIBRA

This is going to be a very dynamic year. You may find out that you are much closer to solving all your problems than you thought earlier.

Job. Career. Throughout the year, you will be moving forward, and whatever happens around, it won't affect your positions. As they say, 'The dogs may bark, but the caravan moves on.'

Despite the worries and bustles around you, you understand what is going on very well and will take the necessary and timely measures.

Contacts with partners from other cities or countries will be especially important; frequent business trips are possible. However, both successes and problems are possible in this sphere. All this has happened before, but this time, there will be more successes and fewer problems.

You will have new allies, who will make it much easier for you to achieve the goals you set.

However, relations with some of your business partners are still far from ideal, serious conflicts are possible, the main reason being real estate, land or some other large property.

You will only achieve what you want at the end of the year, most likely in December. This positive process will continue in 2020.

Those having legal problems may face intrigue and fighting throughout 2019. The result will be clear in December, but it won't be a complete victory as the court will decide in part in your favor and you will lose the other part of your property.

The stars advise the managers and entrepreneurs to be more attentive to the subordinates and monitor their work. It's highly probable that the people you counted on will, in the best-case scenario, be not diligent and incompetent, while in the worst-case scenario, they will turn out to be swindlers and liars.

The employee is advised to be more attentive to the colleagues and avoid intrigue. Many representatives of your sign will be collaborating throughout the year with companies located in other cities or countries. Frequent business trips are possible.

Money. Your financial positions are quite stable throughout the year; no serious changes are expected in this sphere in comparison with 2018.

Love. Family. In 2019, your family life may be uneven and restless. The spouses having a long record of past problems will now have difficulties related to real estate or another large property. In some cases, the problems will result in divorce, which will be a natural consequence of the past problems.

The loving couples will decide to move to a new home or start building a summer house, or even move to another city or country.

2019 will bring you many new acquaintances, which will be good for those who have long been looking for a partner.

Relations with the family members are getting better, your relatives are going through a good period of life and you can rely on them if you have family or professional problems.

Health. In 2019, you are healthy, energetic and quite attractive, which will be obvious for everyone. However, the stars strongly recommend you to be more attentive when traveling and driving. The probability of road accidents and other unpleasant situations is rather high in January, March, June, and September.

SCORPIO

There will be a steady advance in 2019, but you will see both roses and thorns on the road. There is nothing to be done about it, though. This is life!

Job. Career. In terms of job, the year is rather good. What was started in 2018, will be continued in 2019.

A new and wonderful era is coming, the past is rapidly going away. There is no return, you can only move forward.

The circle of your acquaintances is expanding, new people are appearing in your entourage, old ties are being renewed. Relations with old friends as well as with partners living in other cities or countries are getting much better, collaboration agreements are possible. Towards the end of the year, this sphere of your activity can become a major one.

In a number of cases, the developing business or a new job will make you think of relocating, but this is will happen in 2020.

The employee's positions will improve seriously, which will also improve his/her overall financial situation.

Money. The financial sphere looks very good. One can say that most representatives of your sign will rise to a completely different financial level. And this is not a temporary event - positive changes will continue in the next years.

Love. Family. All kinds of events will happen in your personal life. Most couples will find themselves in complicated situations – the partners may have different views on life and different value systems, as well as financial difficulties. In some cases, all this can result in separation.

Many representatives of your sign will resume contacts with their ex-partners living in other cities or countries, which will eventually result in relocation.

Many spouses will have problems with their children: the younger ones may fall ill, while the older ones may behave unreasonably or have personal problems. In either case, a substantial part of the family budget will be spent for the children's needs. In the other version, you will have to pay for your children's education and 'standing on their own feet.' But this is too important to be even discussed - who, if not you?

Relations with some of the relatives are improving, then worsen again. The situation will stabilize towards the end of the year.

Health. During most of the year, your energy potential is not high, so lead a healthy lifestyle and take care of yourself in every possible way. The stars also recommend you to be cautious when traveling and driving.

SAGITTARIUS

For you, 2019 is the beginning of a new cycle. Jupiter, the planet of good luck and new opportunities, will stay in your sign throughout the year, which means that the desired door is open to you!

Job. Career. 2019 may be the best in the last decade for any job-related events.

The entrepreneurs will get new interesting proposals that will raise their business to a higher level. And although many projects may seem unexpected, they are the logical and fair result of the previous 3 or 4 years of hard work and constant anxieties. It's happened at last! Fate is on your side, and life has a lot in store for you.

In 2019, you will have new partners, friends, colleagues and subordinates, who will help you move mountains.

The employee will get a job offer or will be promoted at his/her current company. In either case, everything will be just great!

In terms of job, the best months are February, April, May, August, September, October, and December. The rest of the time, usual problems are inevitable.

Money. Your financial positions will improve in the second half of the year, and a 'golden shower' can be expected in December. For the employee, this is related to a new job, while the entrepreneur will strike extremely successful deals.

Love. Family. While everything is clear and understandable at work in 2019, the situation in your personal life is not that simple. Many spouses have problems in their relationships, such as alienation, misunderstanding, jealousy, or resentment. Everything has changed, new people have appeared around you, and the temptation can be really big.

Many representatives of your sign will have problems with their children at the beginning of the year, which will result in large expenses.

2019 is extremely good for the singles. You can meet someone special, and this relationship has every chance to result in marriage.

Lovers who have been together for quite a while can also decide to get married or start living together.

Many representatives of your sign will have home-related problems, so be careful and prudent, especially if there is already some ambiguity in this sphere.

Health. Throughout the year, your energy potential is very high, so you will stay healthy. The year is good for doing sports as well as for changing the image, including plastic surgery.

CAPRICORN

You always keep everything under your control. But this year, things won't be like that: circumstances beyond your control can be unsettling. And this is equally true for work and for love.

Job. Career. Most representatives of your sign will have to accept that many of the events planned for this year can go much more slowly than planned.

The entrepreneurs and managers will be engaged in reorganization, and, perhaps, expansion of their business. This troublesome work may cause real-estate related problems, as well as complex organizational procedures.

You should also remember that in 2019, you may find yourself under close control of the auditing organs, who can reveal something that you would like to keep secret. Legal problems are also possible.

Those who have foreign connections, will face unpredictable behavior of their foreign colleagues. You will have to understand that your faraway partners are unreliable and their promises can't be trusted. In another variant, your plans will be hampered by some force majeure circumstances, which should also be taken into account.

The employee will face problems inside the team; intrigues, slander and gossip are possible. Also remember that many representatives of your sign can become victims of incorrect, deliberately distorted information. If you want to change your job, take into account that you may have no job offers till December.

The most difficult months will be January, March, June, and September, while October and December will be the best ones.

At the end of the year, Jupiter, the planet of luck, will pass into your sign, which will help you solve all the problems. And the next, 2020, is completely yours! Remember this if you accidentally find yourself under the pressure of the planets.

Money. In terms of finance, this will be an uneven year. This doesn't mean, however, that you won't have money at all, but that most of it will be spent for professional needs or for the needs of your family.

Love. Family. In your personal life, everything is still not easy. Separation is approaching step by step. The problematic couples can understand that they have almost nothing in common and have even nothing to talk about. You will hardly be able to hold what is slipping out of your hands - a new stage is gradually beginning in your life, which means that you will have to part with something and someone. This will not always happen peacefully, especially if there is something to divide.

The stable spouses can spend most of the year trying to resolve various real-estate related issues. Perhaps you will move to another home or start a lengthy renovation or a never-ending construction.

Your children are facing serious changes in their affairs, in general, positive ones. It will only become quite clear at the end of the year, and before that, you should try to understand your children and do your best to help them.

Relations with your relatives will worsen seriously. You may face ingratitude or deceit. Or some of the closest relatives may be ill or have other problems, and you will have to help them with word and deed.

For the lovers, this year is not bad at all. The relationships can progress unexpectedly quickly, but, at the same time, be very uneven. Is the game worth the candle? Of course, it is!

This also refers to the singles who have long been looking for a partner.

Health. Throughout the year, your energy potential is not high, so take care and rest more often. The stars also recommend you to be cautious when traveling and driving.

AQUARIUS

You started from scratch in the recent past. Your life is being gradually filled with new events, new acquaintances, other feelings. There is no way back to the past, you can only move forward.

Job. Career. In 2019, you will be surrounded by people who have power and influence. They will make all your undertakings quite successful. But, at the same time, you can face problems with those people, and, most likely, it will be a matter of finance or other obligations. You may have to give something away, but you will keep a lot. In any case, try to negotiate the terms of collaboration in advance to avoid an embarrassing situation.

However, in general, everything is going on well in your business. Your reputation will improve significantly, the circle of acquaintances will expand, and life will run on cheerfully.

The employee will have the opportunity to get a more interesting and prestigious job, which, most likely, will happen in February. And if this already happened at the end of 2018, he/she have every chance to strengthen his/her positions.

Money. Despite the obvious professional growth, your financial positions are not very stable. On the one hand, you will have more money, but on the other, your expenses will also increase. In one case, this is related to business, and in the other, to personal life.

Love. Family. There are many changes in your personal life. The married people will decide on important acquisitions, such as a new apartment or a summer house. Throughout the year, this decision will be maturing slowly and take shape towards December. In the same period, an unexpected inheritance is likely.

For the lovers, this year is rather complicated. There is a chance of frequent quarrels, distancing and cooling. The most difficult time in this regard is June, July and September. Your relationship seems to hang by a thread, and in one of the difficult months, this thread can break.

Your children require care and attention. As the saying goes, 'the older the children, the bigger the problems.' From time to time, you will spend serious amounts of money for the children's needs.

Health. Throughout the year, your energy potential is rather high. In June and July, however, the stars recommend you to be more careful and avoid potentially dangerous situations. In the same period, exacerbation of chronic illnesses is possible.

pisces

In 2019, you will be a fearless trailblazer, constantly looking for a new peak to conquer. And the stars say that you will find and conquer those peaks.

Job. Career. This year, you will have a lot of opportunities, which you have long dreamed of. The entrepreneurs and managers will start new projects, while the employees can have new jobs.

The planets won't let any professionally active representative of your sign stay where they currently are. If you have perseverance and desire, you will definitely open a new chapter in your life book. This will bring quite new opportunities, both professional and financial. All you need is to concentrate on the main thing, not get confused when having to master some unusual duties, and be able to come to terms with people who occupy high positions inside or outside your current company.

In terms of relations with the boss or high-position persons, June, July and September can be problematic. In these periods, you should look for a compromise in solving the problems, although it won't be easy in some cases. The other 2019 months will be quite OK.

Contacts with the colleagues from other cities or countries will be very important; renewal of old ties and emergence of new business partners are possible. Old friendships will be very important – they can help you move mountains.

Money. Your financial positions will improve greatly, which will be a natural result of a stronger business. April, May, August, November, and December 2019 will be good months for business and finance.

Love. Family. In 2019, your personal life may be less important for you than your job and career. Many representatives of your sign will work round the clock and spend no time with their relatives and loved ones.

This will create inevitable problems, most of which will happen in June, July and September.

In these periods, be more attentive to those who love you and look for compromises in solving all the problems, no matter how difficult it might be in some cases. This advice is equally relevant for lovers and spouses.

The new acquaintances, whose appearance in 2019 is quite probable, can brighten up the lives of the singles and those disappointed in their previous affections. Promising encounters are possible on trips or in the company of those who come from far away.

Health. Throughout the year, your energy potential will be rather high and you will stay healthy.

JANUARY

Aries

In January, the most important things for you are work and career. You are full of energy and don't feel like listening to someone's advice. And still, remember that while in some cases putting pressure on others is quite appropriate, it can do much harm...

Job. Career. Professionally, you can do better than anyone. Now you can tackle the most difficult tasks, so act! There are good opportunities, and you don't want to miss them. A new turn in life is possible for both the employee and the entrepreneur.

Ties with colleagues from other cities and countries are developing actively, a successful business trip is likely.

The entrepreneur will have plans related to the opening of his/her business in places far from his/her home; the employee can count on a new job, and, in some cases, it can have something to do with foreign companies and frequent business trips.

The best time for all professional events is the second and third ten-day periods of January, when the solar and lunar eclipses will help you advance your plans and projects.

However, despite the obvious success, the stars advise you to be more attentive in your business agreements. It is possible that proposals that look good have hidden pitfalls, which you should pay close attention to. A little later, in March, June and September, they can come to the surface and cause a lot of problems. So don't ignore any vague details, think twice, discuss the peculiarities and, if possible, put them on paper.

A wonderful period begins for students and for those who are eager to learn something new. The stars offer a "green light" for new twists and turns and don't advise anyone to stay where they presently are.

Money. The financial situation is stable, with a clear tendency to improve. Favorable opportunities open one after another; the lucky ones can expect quick profits as soon as in January, others - a little later.

Love. Family. In your personal life, avoid hasty decisions and categorical judgments. The most difficult time is the period from January 20 through 27, when the probability of conflicts is very high.

The spouses having difficulties in their personal life as well as dissatisfied lovers are going to have a tough conversation about the future of their relationship; it won't be easy to answer questions asked by life.

Look for a compromise and don't pull the blanket over yourself – that's the only way to improve the situation and get out of the labyrinth of problems.

Traveling can help reduce tension in the relationship - try to spend the January holidays together, preferably somewhere far from home.

People who live alone can expect an interesting encounter, and it is possible that it will take place on a trip or in a circle of people who come from far away.

Health. In January, you are energetic, healthy and enterprising, but the stars strongly advise you to be more careful on trips and while driving. In this respect, the most difficult period is January 10 through 15.

TAURUS

In January, the stars advise you not to make haste. Take decisions and act only if you are fully confident in the outcome. Your motto should be "The quieter you go, the further you will get."

Job. Career. In January, the solar and lunar eclipses can call you on a trip or make you intensify contacts with colleagues from other cities and countries. Those who are planning to expand their business in another city or country can make important steps in that direction.

Real estate operations will be successful, including acquiring, exchanging, and selling.

However, relations with faraway partners can develop unevenly. Unexpected problems will arise in the third tenday period of January; you must be ready for them in advance. There will be manifestations of the future problems, so please pay close attention to those indications.

People having legal problems can face more obstacles, and in this respect, the third tenday period of January is also unfavorable.

In the same unlucky period, the bosses and the entrepreneurs are advised to get ready for unexpected checks.

Another problem of this month will be relations with certain friends or so-called "patrons". It is unlikely that they should be counted on, because a little later it will become clear that their promises remain just promises. And this is the best-case scenario; in the worst-case one, deception is possible.

The employee is advised to be more attentive to his/her duties and, if possible, avoid intrigue. Otherwise, you can get into a difficult situation and be accused of the problems you never created.

Money. Money can also be a problem this month. A lot of expenses should be expected, and in one case they will be related to business, while in the other - to rest, home and family needs. However, you can rely on the help of your loved ones or business partners. Many of you will profit from successful real estate operations.

Love. Family. There will be many changes in your private life. Spouses who have good relations with each other will continue improving their city house, apartment or summer house, which will make the family life quite busy.

Many will have trouble with their relatives. A loved one can get sick or experience some trouble; a serious quarrel is highly possible.

Those in love can experience alienation, their relationship will become cooler. In some cases, this may be caused by someone's intrigue, so prefer listening to talking, and don't give cause for gossip. This advice is relevant for all representatives of your sign, regardless of age and type of activity.

Health. In January, your energy potential is low, so take care of yourself and be moderate.

Drivers and travelers should be especially cautious. Traumatic and conflict time is the third tenday period of the month, especially January 20 through 24.

GEMINI

January is not the best time for moving forward, it is better to focus on something you know well. It's time to strengthen the rear!

Job. Career. January is not very good for your profession. And it's not just the Christmas and New Year holidays, but the fact that this month is traditionally unsuccessful for you. All representatives of your sign, regardless of the nature of their work, should pay attention to their entourage, since problems are likely - both moral and financial.

In particular, it will not be easy for the employee to find a common language with his boss; misunderstandings and even reprimands from the boss are possible.

The entrepreneurs will have to word more clearly the objectives of their business to avoid misunderstandings with their business partners.

There is a high probability of disagreements with friends or certain superiors about money or other material values.

At the same time, relations with some partners will be quite harmonious; it is possible that, in difficult situations, you can count on their help, both moral and financial.

Money. For you, January is a month of spending. Expenses will be the backdrop of the whole month, the largest of them will be made in the third tenday period of January. In one case, they will be related to business, in another one, to personal life. Holidays, travel, children's needs - all this can require a lot of money. But, as they say, "miser pays twice", so pamper yourself and your loved ones if you can afford it.

However, at the end of the month, be careful with money and other valuables, since the probability of losses is very high at this time.

This advice is especially important for brokers, bankers, accountants, and everyone whose activities have something to do with finances.

Love. Family. In the love relationship, the situation changes almost every day. Quarrels alternate with reconciliation, but there is a hope that, in the end, love will win.

Venus, Mars, and Jupiter are actively in contact, which means that the love affairs are booming; many have plans related to marriage or cohabitation.

Loving couples have good relationships; your spouse will succeed, which will make you happy.

Health. This month, your energy potential is low, so take advantage of the Christmas and New Year holidays and have a good rest.

Elderly people and those suffering osseous system's illnesses should be especially careful: this month, the probability of exacerbations is quite high. Besides, there is a chance of injuries and accidents in the second half of the month. Everyone must take this into account, including those who prefer active and extreme types of rest.

CANCER

Creativity and sense of humor will help you cope with any difficulties in January. Patience will let you avoid conflicts in situations when someone close to you will behave differently than planned and dreamed about.

Job. Career. Despite the Christmas and New Year holidays, you will do a lot. There will be plenty of work to do, and in this respect, representatives of your sign will be ahead of all others.

The entrepreneurs and the bosses can safely rely on their subordinates; the employees can count on their colleagues.

However, in any "barrel of honey there is a fly in the ointment". This time, it will be your relations with some of your business partners. Perhaps, it will be about the past, but this time, the opponents' claims will be more rigid and more specific. The reasons for all that will be different views on the development of the whole business or its part.

There will be difficulties developing contacts with colleagues from other cities and countries: in this sphere, unclear, intricate situations or direct deception are possible. So take your time, act slowly and carefully, until all the details of the future project are quite clear.

But, despite numerous difficulties, your business will go forward, and there will be those who will help and support you. You will have new opportunities, new directions and, some time later, this will bring you a good income.

Money. Financial situation is quite stable, money will be received regularly, and its amount will increase significantly. The largest amounts can be expected on January 22 through 31.

Love. Family. While there is a significant progress in your work, you experience problems in your personal life. The severe Saturn, firmly established in the sky sector in charge of partnership, requires patience and a responsible attitude towards the loved one. Intercooling can even be experienced by very amicable couples; those who have long been living in a state of stress and quarrels will be close to divorce.

Violent conflicts are expected towards the end of the month and, perhaps, one of them will be the final one. Remember this, and even when quarreling, try to keep a sober perception of the situation.

Another option is that your loved one can get sick or have another kind of trouble and thus need help and support.

Experienced couples are also likely to face such problems.

Health. In terms of health, January is not bad at all - this is the most suitable time to take care of yourself. A sanatorium, a good hotel, a visit to a spa, sauna or hammam - all such activities will bring you obvious benefits. If you want to do sports, this is the best time.

LEO

In January, you will do your best to make others feel confident and comfortable. And a positive reaction will not keep you waiting!

Job. Career. In January, you will be "working like a dog", with all the corresponding consequences.

A lot of routine work is expected, but this is a necessary condition for further progress. The bosses and the entrepreneurs must pay attention to their subordinates; certain disagreements are likely in regard with unfulfilled obligations and unfinished business.

Relations with colleagues from other cities and countries will be developing with varied success, both achievements and problems are likely.

In general, the situation is positive, but there are moments that require discussion and refinement.

The most difficult time is the last ten days of January, when serious misunderstandings and conflicts are likely.

The most productive time is the second tenday period of the month, when it will be possible to solve some problems and improve the situation a little.

Those who have legal problems are also advised to take the necessary measures in the second, most successful tenday period of the month.

Business trips planned for this period will be rather successful.

Money. With regard to finance, January can develop unevenly. The astrologer believes that the main expenses will relate to your family and domestic affairs; a lot of money will be spent for the children.

In general, the financial sphere needs special control, and this should be taken into account by all representatives of this sign and especially by those whose work is directly connected with money and other material values.

Love. Family. In January, you will depend completely on the people surrounding you. You will do your best for your loved ones.

Those who have families will be happy with their children's successes; a favorable period will continue for the children. In many families, the appearance of offspring is likely. At the same time, it will be necessary in the middle of the month to allocate serious money for the needs of the younger generation, and it will be much more than originally expected.

For those in love, January is also not bad. A joint trip is possible, which will help strengthen the relationship. The best time for this is the first and second tenday periods of January.

The third ten days are hard in all respects, so planning long trips is not recommended for this period.

Relations with the loved ones are not easy; in all probability, the problem is your spouse's relatives. Sharp conflicts are likely in the third tenday period of January and, if they cannot be avoided, be happy with the fact that "all the t's will be crossed".

Health. January is a good time for taking care of yourself. If you can't go to a warm sea, try to spend more time in the countryside, do sports, or just walk. This is a good period for doing cosmetics and massage, going to a sauna or a Russian bath.

In the third ten days of the month, be careful when traveling and driving!

VIRGO

January is a calm, cozy, "home" month. It is a surprisingly good time for arranging your housing and strengthening relationships with your loved ones.

Job. Career. Incorrigible workaholics as well as many of those born under your sign can dedicate January to serious organizational work. Entrepreneurs and superiors can move to a new office or renovate the old one completely.

Many will think about opening their own business and finding a suitable place for it.

The employee will spend most of January working about the house, and for this reason his/her vacation is likely to last.

The biggest problem in January will be your relations with your business partners: conflicts, misunderstandings or even deception are possible.

Most likely, it will be about finances or other material values, but everything is not so bad - after tense negotiations, it will be possible to come to terms.

The most difficult time is the third tenday period of January, when the disagreements will reach their peak. Be patient, get ready for this as well as for the fact that part of the funds will have to be given away.

Money. The financial situation is not quite stable in January. Income is not likely, while expenses are inevitable. They will be related to paying off old debts and credits, or to the needs of the family, and, above all, the children.

Love. Family. If you are planning to do something good for your family and loved ones, this is the best time. Big changes in everyday life are likely, such as moving to a new house or a complete renovation of the interior.

At the same time, relations with the spouse are not ideal, and it's not about you - all the misunderstandings possible in the second and third tenday periods of January are caused by the unpredictable and detached attitude of your partner. It is possible that he/she is hiding something from you or deceives you in some way.

Children, as it often happens, will cause big expenses, and some of the latter will turn out to be quite unexpected. Be especially attentive to the elders, perhaps now they are more than usual in need of your support and attention.

The lovers will have a difficult time: much can change in the relationship, and not for the better.

The influence of eclipses on the sky sector responsible for your love affairs will require restraint and circumspection from you. Otherwise, any conflict can have far-reaching consequences.

The astrologer advises you not to demand too much from the partner, and especially in the material sphere.

Health. This month, your energy potential will be high enough, but there will be a high probability of gaining weight, so be more restrained in eating and drinking.

LIBRA

January is a great time to get away and do what you want. "All work and no play will make one dull!". For you, the playtime has come at last!

Job. Career. The first tenday period of January is unproductive, and for you, the main reason is the holidays. The second and third tenday periods are more active, while both good luck and problems are probable.

Relations with faraway colleagues develop, in general, in the right direction, but it should be noted that not all the partners are reliable and not all the promises should be trusted. Some misunderstandings are likely in the middle of the month, when it will become clear that much in the relationship needs to be specified and clarified.

Besides, bosses should pay attention to their subordinates, who may be slow, lazy, and even capable of deception.

The third tenday period of January is a time of conflict, there may be disagreements with some of your ex-partners, related to a big property, maybe land or another real estate.

There is no quick solution, so be patient and defend your position step by step.

Money. This month, the financial situation is unstable, mostly because of the holidays, the needs of the family and your loved ones. Insignificant income is possible on January 19, 20, 27-29.

Love. Family. The severe Saturn is firmly entrenched in the sky sector responsible for family life, which means that you are having problems in this area. Even loving couples can quarrel more often than usual, and those whose relationships are already tough can think seriously about divorce.

In all respects, the most difficult time is the third tenday period of January, when the probability of conflicts is very high. The solar and lunar eclipses will put many before the choice - family or work, and make them balance between these important spheres, which is hard to do. Something else is also possible: it is your partner who will have to make a similar choice.

The separating couples will raise again the issue of real estate, but they will hardly find a solution this month.

Traveling will help improve the situation. If you travel to distant lands together and forget, at least temporarily, about mutual accusations, your relationship will improve greatly.

People who are alone and disappointed in their previous relationships can count on a fateful encounter on a trip or in a circle of people who come from far away.

Relations with the relatives will improve significantly; in difficult situations, you can count on the support of your loved ones, whose business is getting better.

Health. This month, your energy potential is low, so use the Christmas and New Year holidays for a full rest, countryside walks, relaxing at the seaside, and reading good books.

SCORPIO

The motto of this month is flexibility. Faced with obstacles, think about detours and in no case go baldheaded.

Job. Career. Despite the Christmas and New Year holidays, you will do a lot and succeed in everything related to money and business.

There will be a lot of work. In addition to the old projects, you can count on new proposals, very good professionally and financially. The most productive time is the second tenday period of January, when you can move mountains.

However, luck is rarely complete, and this will be the case this time, too. The stumbling block will be the difficult relations with your colleagues from other cities and countries: there can be travel delays, unpredictable behavior of the business partners, or problems with documents. So-called "force majeure" situations are also possible.

The peak of all problems will be in the third tenday period of January, which will be the most difficult period of the month.

Money. The financial situation this month is quite stable. The money will be received regularly and its amount will increase significantly. The approximate dates for receiving the largest amounts are January 2-4, 12, 13, 21-23, 30, 31.

This month's expenses will be related mostly to the personal sphere - the children and the loved ones.

Love. Family. Personal life in January will not be very stable. The lovers will be quarreling, the probable cause being financial claims. There may also be misunderstandings, different world outlooks and value systems, which will make one look at the relationship from a new angle and affect it seriously.

Those married can take care of the children's problems and spend substantial amounts of money for their needs.

Relations with the relatives are far from ideal - serious quarrels are possible, and in some cases, this will lead to separation and termination of the relations.

In another situation, relatives can experience hard time and you will have to help them with word and deed.

Health. In January, your energy potential is low, so lead a healthy lifestyle and take care of yourself in every possible way.

The car drivers and the travelers are advised to be more careful - the probability of accidents and other unpleasant situations is high enough.

In this respect, the most difficult time is the third tenday period of the month. During this period, the stars recommend you to abandon all trips, both close and distant, since they will only bring you problems.

SAGITTARIUS

Jupiter is in your sign, which means that everything is available to you! A great time for starting big, long-term projects, and a great love story, too!

Job. Career. The main event in the professional life of most representatives of your sign will be relations with colleagues from other cities and countries. And even the Christmas and New Year holidays can be devoted to these important events, which will have a good and, perhaps, fateful continuation.

For all professional matters, the best time is the second tenday period of January, when you can count on a successful business trip and meetings with people who will provide all possible support to your projects.

Remember that no matter how long and complicated those projects are, you will definitely have enough strength and patience to complete them.

Special success awaits the people of creative professions - their ideas will be universally recognized, and many will get deserved though unexpected popularity.

Money. In terms of finance, January can be uneven. Money will be received regularly and its amount will increase significantly. However, as it often happens, expenses will also increase. This will be related to travel, business investments, or the needs of the family, loved ones, or children.

And, in many cases, the expenses can be excessive and not quite reasonable.

Love. Family. The influence of Jupiter is favorable for those whose interests are focused on personal life. The circle of acquaintances will expand noticeably, which is a good opportunity to rearrange their lives. Fate will give you new opportunities, which will come in handy to those who spent a lot of time looking for a partner.

Those who have a permanent partner can also succumb to the temptation of change, but if there is no desire to destroy what is already available, it is better to direct the sky energy to strengthening the old union.

In a word, the stars give you many opportunities and it's up to you to use them.

In the family life, many pleasant events can be related to your children, but it is possible that a large amount of money from the family budget will be spent for their needs.

Health. In January, you are active and healthy, but those who have a bone system disease or a motor system disease, should take care of themselves. For many representatives of your sign, yoga would do a lot of good.

CAPRICORN

In January, your energy can be directed to your home, family and loved ones. The influence of eclipses will make you establish "your rules of the game".

Job. Career. In terms of profession, January is not very effective.

And the problem is not just the Christmas and New Year holidays, but the fact that the interests of home and family will be more important for you. The exception is incorrigible workaholics, as well as those whose activities are related to real estate. In this sphere, nothing will prevent you from achieving success.

All organizational arrangements, such as putting things in order in the old office or moving to new premises, will be rather successful.

Be restrained and careful in dealing with your business partners, and remember that you can also be wrong. Now, more than ever, you can be characterized as a stubborn and selfish person, which will negatively affect your relations with the partners.

Money. The sphere of finance is quite predictable and stable. Successful operations with real estate, obtaining a credit on favorable terms, financial support of business partners are possible. Those who have nothing to do with business can rely on the help of their loved ones.

Love. Family. In personal life, this is the time of change. The loving families can leave their former habitations and move to new ones. In another situation, there is a big renovation or a complete change of the old interior.

At the same time, relations with the loved ones are far from ideal, and the problem is, of course, you, your desire to do everything and make decisions without taking into account the opinions of your loved ones. Your soul needs a change, but this is not a reason to get on the nerves of those who have long cared about your happiness and comfort.

The influence of Uranus, the planet of change, will make you rush from one side to another: it is possible that a new love story will make you revise many things, but even in this case, nothing will prevent you from being impeccable in relation to your former attachments.

Health. This month, your energy potential is somewhat reduced, and special caution is recommended to those who have chronic problems with the bone system and the spine. Of all sports, the most useful for you now are yoga and all kinds of stretching. A relaxing massage will help you sooth your nerves.

AQUARIUS

January can be a month of family and home. This period is not too good for working, but it is good for strengthening relationships with your loved ones.

Job. Career. In the first tenday period of the month, there will be "silence" in business. This is most naturally related to the Christmas and New Year holidays, and in your case, the holidays can be somewhat extended. However, nothing prevents you from spending your vacation together with your friends and discussing current affairs and future plans. You will definitely have such opportunities in January.

Contacts with colleagues from other cities and countries are activated, a trip is possible as well as meetings with friends or persons occupying high positions in the society. In this respect, the most successful time is the second tenday period of January.

In the third tenday period, the positive effects of cosmos will be alternating whimsically with negative ones, that is, some unexpected problems will be solved quickly and effectively "with a little help from your friends" or support of high patrons. In general, you are doing well and this month is good for communication, as well as for acquiring new business-related ties.

Money. With regard to finance, January can develop unevenly. Money will be received regularly, but the expenses will increase, too, so at the end of January, your balance may turn out to be negative. The largest amount can go away in the middle of the month and, perhaps, it will be related to one of the friends or to the needs of the patrons.

Perhaps it will be necessary to solve problems of a legal nature or report to the inspecting authorities.

The stars strongly encourage you to pay attention to money and keep all your financial documents in order. A kind of chaos, to which you will be inclined, will certainly lead to losses, which could be avoided.

Love. Family. In personal life, various situations are possible. Many families will face problems with relatives and they may be sick or go through bad times; besides, a serious quarrel is likely. The stars advise you to take care of your older relatives in any way possible. In this respect, the whole of January is complicated, especially its last ten days.

The lovers can be either separated from each other or, for different reasons, not meet as often as they would like to. The stars recommend them as well as "experienced" spouses to forget about all kinds of problems for some time, escape from the routine and everyday worries. Love is a tender and fragile flower, and it can easily fade without being taken care of on a regular basis.

Health. This month, your energy potential is low, which will be especially noticeable in New Moon and eclipses on January 5-7. Reduce your activeness these days and devote all your time to yourself.

The car drivers and the travelers are also advised to be more careful and discreet. It would be better not to go on trips, both close and distant.

Also, the traumatic days of the month are January 8, 12, 18, 19, 23.

pisces

January promises to be a noisy, joyful and "expensive" month. Dream big and celebrate big!

Job. Career. Besides the well-deserved rest, January will bring you many professional growth opportunities. The entrepreneurs will manage to continue the important project launched last fall, and the employees will strengthen their positions doing a new project.

Those who, in the recent past, negotiated another application of their talents can count on a positive decision in the second half of January.

Luck is on the side of those who are not afraid to take a step forward and are ready to work hard for that.

In January, you can do things together with your old friends, but the relations with them must be built on the principle that "money has nothing to do with friendship." That is, all obligations and agreements must be discussed and documented in order to avoid problems in the future.

This advice is also relevant for the people who decided to use the services of those occupying higher positions.

Money. The financial situation is quite unstable. Money will be received regularly and its amount will increase significantly. However, as is often the case, expenses will also increase.

Try to control your surroundings and don't lend money – or you will lose both money and friends.

The largest amounts can be expected on January 3, 4, 12-14, 21-23. Most of the expenses are to be expected in the third tenday period of the month.

Love. Family. Surprisingly, social, friendly and professional contacts will be more significant in January than personal and romantic ones.

However, this doesn't imply problems in love affairs, it rather means that people close to you will support your endeavors and take part, together with you, in the stormy life events.

The married people will take care of their children's matters and do a lot for their advancement and development.

Here is what the stars advise you: When doing something for yourself, don't forget that there are people who need your help. A kind word and a smile will help you solve a lot of problems - remember this as well as the fact that the most difficult time is the third tenday period of the month.

Health. In January, your energy potential is high enough and you are not afraid of falling ill.

FEBRUARY

ARIES

This month, you will know for sure what to do and how to do it. More than that, your friends will know what they should do for you; now you can lean on their strong shoulders.

Job. Career. In February, the main trend is further improvement of relations with your colleagues living in other cities and countries. There is a chance of a trip, meeting new business partners and general expansion of your circle of acquaintances.

This month, contacts with friends living in other cities and countries will be very important in all your undertakings. Friendly ties can facilitate your tasks greatly and move things forward. If you want change, February is a good time for it.

It is possible that people occupying high social positions will take part in your business; their support can also play a positive role in advancing it.

The employees can expect promotion or, as a more modest option, they will be praised by the boss. A small bonus is also likely.

Money. This month, money will become something regular and its amount will somewhat increase. The employee can have a salary raise, or his achievements can be marked somehow. The self-employed person can count on profitable deals. Estimated dates for receiving the most significant amounts are February 1-3, 11, 12, 21, 22.

Love. Family. This month, most of your time will again be devoted to work, so it's possible that you won't have any time for private life.

The only exception is couples whose life and work are interrelated, as well as those planning to have a so-called "office romance." As to the rest of the people, the stars advise you to be more attentive to your partner and try to explain to him/her why you are always busy at work.

If you plan a business trip, it would be a good idea to travel with your regular partner. If this is impossible, write or call her/him as often as you can. This will help you avoid misunderstanding and resentment.

Health. This month, your energy potential is high enough and you will be quite healthy. But after February 19, you will feel tired due to the previous activity, so you will need some rest. The stars advise you to listen to your body, reduce activity and sleep well.

TAURUS

February is a month of activity and success. And although your major achievements are still ahead, you can now achieve a lot, too.

Job. Career. This month, you can face a professional dilemma: leave the past behind and take up a new job, or stay where you are now?

The astrologer believes that someone will have to solve the problem right away, while others may do it later. In any case, it makes sense to take a closer look at the proposals that you will most probably have in February.

Relations with colleagues from other cities and countries are OK; a trip is possible, and it will be quite successful in all aspects.

The stars still recommend you to be careful when communicating with your friends and not trust their promises very much. Try to control the situation and especially the financial sphere. Similar recommendations will be vital for those who, for various reasons, are connected by business relations or obligations with people of a higher social status. Remember that what was promised will not necessarily be fulfilled!

This month, constructors and all those whose business has something to do with real estate or agriculture can count on successful deals and stable progress of their business.

Money. Your financial positions are unchanged, and there is an obvious tendency for improvement. A good profit is probable due to successful operations with real estate as well as support of your business partners or loved ones.

February expenses can still be related to the unstable position of one of your friends or people who occupy a high social position. The astrologer advises you not to lend money and control the expenses made by your entourage.

Love. Family. In family life, what began in the past will continue in February. For example, many people will succeed in improving their housing: someone will look for a new house, others will buy furniture or do serious renovation. In some cases, those worrisome events will take place in another city or country.

It is hard to say something definite about the lovers. Changes in their relationships are unlikely, but, maybe, some couples will try to live together.

Health. This month, your energy potential is quite high and you are not afraid of falling ill. The women have a high probability of pregnancy and, if this is not among your plans, please take all necessary precautions.

GEMINI

February is the month of movement and changes. And whose will be positive changes indeed!

Job. Career. February promises growth. It can be an expansion of the communication circle, more respect from the colleagues, friends and acquaintances. There is a chance of a trip, meetings with colleagues from other cities and countries; you can have new acquaintances and business partners.

Despite a significant improvement in the situation, there are still numerous unresolved business issues. For example, the entrepreneurs will have to determine the specific goals and objectives of their business, as well as find a common language with their business partners.

The employee will partially regulate his/her relations with the boss, but please remember that you are still far from mutual understanding. However, "the road is made by walking", and if you make some effort, you will see, towards the end of February, that this proverb is quite true.

Money. Despite the improvement in business, no significant financial improvement is expected. February won't bring you a big income, but there will be no losses either. Looking ahead, the situation will improve in March. In some cases, the improvement can be expected in late February.

Love. Family. There is a significant revival in your personal life. The lovers have stable relationships, and there is a clear positive tendency. The quarrelling couples will find a good reason for reconciliation. Many will think about getting married and travelling together.

The unmarried people can meet an interesting person in February, and this encounter will, in some cases, be fateful.

The "experienced" spouses will be able to strengthen their relationship and forget about the recent quarrels.

Trips scheduled for February will be very successful, so if you have time, take your loved one with you and hit the road.

Health. This month, you are healthy, energetic and able to make a good impression on everyone you come across.

CANCER

In February, don't hurry up to make decisions, and take good care assessing your possibilities. Do your best to accept other people's points of view, and be prepared for compromises.

Job. Career. February is very good for all kinds of organizational arrangements and putting things in order. This is quite necessary, because new directions that have just appeared in your business will require careful preparation.

The entrepreneurs and managers may need a serious business reorganization to implement the new spheres of activity.

The employee can receive new assignments or negotiate a new job. Somewhat later, you will certainly be a success, but for now, you have time to think it over again.

Relations with your colleagues from other cities and countries still need special control. If you are serious about collaboration, ask your old friends to help you, and they will help stabilize the situation.

Money. In terms of finance, this month is more or less neutral. Big income can't be expected, and the expenses are quite predictable and reasonable. At the same time, February is good for negotiations concerning sponsorship, credit, and financial support from your business partners.

Those who have nothing to do with businesses can get help from parents or a loved one.

Love. Family. In personal life, everything is relatively calm. Your relationship will stabilize and warm up. The quarreling spouses and lovers will have a good opportunity to understand their problems and meet each other halfway. This year, there are not many such opportunities, so please don't miss your chance!

The unmarried people will have the opportunity to turn old friendships into something more significant, and, over time, those relationships will last for years.

Health. In February, your energy potential is not particularly stable, so, despite being very busy, find time for having a rest. Be especially cautious in New Moon, i.e. on February 3 through 5: during this period, you can be at the very bottom of life activity. So don't take chances – try to avoid all kinds of excesses, and take good care of yourself!

LEO

Be ready to compromise and accept other people's views. If you do this, February will bring you a lot of nice minutes and let you achieve a lot.

Job. Career. In February, the main achievement is developing old ties and acquiring new ones. If you make an effort, you can get support from your entourage and advance your business seriously.

Development of ties with your colleagues from other cities and countries is possible, as well as a successful business trip.

It is also possible that you will resume working on old projects and negotiate on this matter with your former business partners, colleagues and subordinates. It is also possible that, in the nearest future, the project you considered finalized will find a new life, but on a different and more solid basis.

The employee can resume negotiations on the previous job or involve his/her ex- colleagues in a new project. In all cases, please remember that moving to something new is only possible on the well-established old base.

Money. Financially, February can be uneven. Big expenses can be related to your children or loved ones, and in some cases, they will exceed your expectations significantly.

In the second half of the month, negotiations are possible on credit, sponsorship, and financial support from your business partners.

Those people who have nothing to do with business can rely on the help from their loved ones.

Love. Family. February is very good for your personal life. In the relationship, serious progress is possible as the "love" sectors in your map are lit favorably by both Sun and Jupiter. The stars promise you new acquaintances that will expand your communication circle. Fate will open up unplanned opportunities for you, which will come in handy, especially for those who have long been looking for a partner.

This month, you can meet a person who will be easy and fun to communicate with. Eventually, this can grow into something more serious and significant.

The married people will be happy with their children's successes, but a decent share of the family budget will be spent for their needs.

More often than not, an addition to the family is quite possible.

Health. For most of February, your energy potential is high enough, and only the last tenday period of the month will bring you weakness and fatigue. Take care of yourself and try to find time for rest and full sleep.

In February, the women have a high probability of pregnancy.

VIRGO

In February, star influence will allow you to get under way and start writing a new page of your professional biography. Use this chance before you find yourself at a crossroads again!

Job. Career. In terms of professional activity, this month is quite favorable. You will have an opportunity to stabilize your complex partnership relations, so don't miss that opportunity.

A certain tension is still likely though as your partners are still unpredictable and it is hardly possible to predict what they are going to do next. However, your business is moving forward: negotiations on finance are successful; by mid February, you will be able to contact your colleagues from other cities or countries and reach agreement on issues important for you.

The employee will do much in cooperation with his/her colleagues and somewhat improve his/her position. Although you can't expect big achievements, every step forward is incredibly valuable for you. As the saying goes, "Patience always pays back", which is absolutely true in your case.

Money. Your financial situation will somewhat improve, but it can't be called quite stable. For some, their February expenses will be related to paying off the old debts, for others, to the needs of the family and, above all, the children.

However, your income will also increase, so you will probably be able to keep a positive balance.

The estimated dates of getting the largest amounts are February 4, 5, 14, 15, 22, 23.

Love. Family. In personal life, quite controversial events are possible.

The "experienced" lovers can have a serious quarrel in the early days of February, but then their relationship will improve, and the second half of the month will be quite calm.

The married people will have problems with their children, which will result in large expenses. The "experienced" spouses will have problems reaching mutual understanding and, for various reasons, they may drift apart.

In many families, activity related to real estate will continue and be the reason of the family problems.

Health. February is ideal for sports, massage and other health-oriented activities. Don't be lazy, especially if you tend to gain weight, which is the case with many representatives of your sign.

LIBRA

More changes are underway. You are facing your future boldly, and February will give you another chance to change your life. For the better, of course!

Job. Career. Being active, charming and eloquent will make it possible for you to become a real center of attraction during the whole month. This is a great time for gaining supporters and allies, strengthening old ties and finding new ones.

Contacts with colleagues from other cities and countries are developing more or less well, frequent business trips and fruitful negotiations are possible.

Certain disagreements dating back to the distant and recent past may still remind you of themselves, but the positive tendencies are more numerous, and there is no doubt that they will continue in the future. Be sure of this and overcome the inevitable obstacles step by step.

The bosses and the entrepreneurs are still recommended to pay attention to their subordinates. The latter may be not diligent and incompetent. If you don't keep your team under control, the problems will multiply and hamper your business seriously. In the most difficult case, one of those who is supposed to do what he/she is told and support you, can simply deceive you.

Money. In terms of finance, February is more likely to be neutral, although much money can be spent for the so-called "hospitality" requirements, entertainment, and children. However, you have enough money and, towards the end of the month, will be able to keep a positive balance.

Love. Family. There is no doubt that romantic feelings are difficult to "plan", but do keep in mind that February is a great time for entertainment, making friends, moonlight walks and other pleasures of life.

The unmarried people can expect having new acquaintances, and there is a high probability that this will happen on a trip or in a circle of people who came from far away.

At the very beginning of the month, the married people can have a serious quarrel, the main reason being domestic affairs and certain unresolved real estate issues. The divorcing couples will face similar problems.

The children will mostly make you happy; many representatives of your sign will have the opportunity to spend more time with them than usual.

Any trips scheduled for February will be very successful.

Health. This month, you are full of energy and won't fall ill. If you feel like going to the gym or master new kinds of sports, this is the best time.

SCORPIO

This month, don't overestimate your abilities and don't take on too much responsibility. Don't go beyond the limits in all matters you have to tackle.

Job. Career. In February, you will focus on your job and making money, and this will bring fruit. You can aim at new directions and involve new people in your business.

The entrepreneurs and the bosses will have new assistants; the employees will have new colleagues.

Relations with your colleagues from other cities and countries will somewhat improve, but they can't be called quite stable. At the beginning of the month, significant complications are possible, which will only be settled in the second tenday period.

Many representatives of your sign have to do a lot of organizational work, as well as various real estate operations. In February, all such undertakings will be very successful.

Money. Financially, this month is very successful. Money will be received regularly and its amount will increase significantly.

The estimated dates for receiving the most substantial amounts are February 9, 10, 18, 19, 26, 27. This month's expenses are still related to your children or loved ones.

Love. Family. In February, many representatives of your sign will pay a lot of attention to their homes and families. Everyday life changes are possible, such as home improvement and renovation, the most ambitious option being acquisition of a new house/apartment or making the corresponding plans.

Relations with your relatives will be somewhat better, but it seems that the long-standing grievances are impossible to resolve overnight. In many cases, the children will point the way to reconciliation; their influence will help you meet each other halfway.

At the same time, the children's needs will require a serious amount of money from the family budget, but what can be more important?

The lovers can think about living together; in this case, they will take certain steps in this direction. Support from their parents will be priceless.

Health. In February, your energy potential is not very high. Besides, there can be a tendency to gain weight, so you must have a sense of proportion, both in eating and drinking. Go to the gym more often, and fast one day a week.

SAGITTARIUS

The planets line up in a happy row, which means that everything will be your way in February, in terms of work and love.

Job. Career. In February, many representatives of your sign will spend most of the time outside their homes. Trips, meetings, negotiations will make the main background of this month. Intensive contacts are possible with colleagues from other cities and countries as well as collaboration proposals with good perspectives for the future.

The employee will receive an additional assignment, probably implying a business trip. Your professional positions will improve, and this will affect your finances in a positive way.

February is also successful for studying and gaining new knowledge as well as for any plans related to life renewal. Success also awaits people of creative professions - they can go on an exciting and bright tour.

The advice to all representatives of this trouble-causing sign is to take up all proposals boldly, no matter how risky they may seem: Jupiter's support is huge, and it will help you do a lot!

Money. Business success will improve your financial position. Getting money will become a regular phenomenon in February, and its amount will increase significantly.

The estimated dates for receiving the most substantial amounts are February 1, 2, 11-13, 20, 21, 24, 25.

There will be few expenses in February, all of them being predictable and reasonable.

Love. Family. There is a difference between the lovers and the spouses. The former will be lucky, of course: February will be an interesting and happy month for them, they will spend it in complete unity with each other.

A somewhat different relationship may develop between the spouses, especially those whose relationships have long been complicated and confusing. Financial claims are possible, as well as serious disagreements related to the children or the common house/apartment. They will hardly be solved this month; most likely this will be delayed at least for half a year.

Relations with relatives will improve significantly; meetings with relatives living in another city or country are possible.

Any trips scheduled for February will be successful, so, if you want to travel, do hit the road!

As to the unmarried people, the stars advise you to attend parties and socialize as much as possible as this is a great time to meet someone you really need.

Health. In February, you are healthy, energetic and very attractive, which will be noticed by everyone you meet with.

CAPRICORN

February is good for solving big legal and financial problems. Things will go in the right direction.

Job. Career. This month, you have everything to establish yourself as an excellent leader and organizer.

The entrepreneurs and the bosses will have successful real estate deals, be it buying, renovation or selling.

Relations with colleagues from other cities or countries are developing with varying success. These areas of activity still need your vigilant control. Don't let your colleagues and subordinates do it instead of you. Nothing but your firm hand will clarify your foreign colleagues' attitude. Do everything by yourself, and you will succeed!

This advice also relates to those who have legal problems or claims from the audit authorities.

The employee is advised to pay attention to people around him/her and avoid any intrigues.

The incoming information should be checked carefully as it may be inaccurate or unreliable. This is true for all representatives of your sign, regardless of their activity, especially those who plan to travel abroad in late February or in March.

Money. It will be the focus of your attention most of February, and for good reason. You will have much more money; the estimated dates for receiving the largest amounts are February 4, 5, 14, 15, 22, 23, 24, 25. There will be various reasons for that.

Love. Family. Venus is in your sign, which means that people are fond of you.

There is a chance of an interesting continuation of an old romance, which has begun and stopped more than once. Now your personal life will go on more smoothly, but everything mainly depends on you.

It's usually hard for you to speak about your feelings, preferences and desires, which creates certain difficulties for your partner. Remember this and try to be more responsive.

The married people whose life is stable are engaged in important matters related to arranging their homes. In February, this will go on smoothly, without delays or problems.

Relations with your relatives are still complicated, but your efforts can play a role and change the situation for the better.

Health. In February, your energy potential is not very high, but if you lead a healthy lifestyle, you won't fall ill.

AQUARIUS

You are moving steadily towards your goal, and February will allow you to take one more step forward. The secret of your success lies in your self-confidence and clear understanding of your wishes and goals.

Job. Career. During the whole month, you will be extremely energetic and enthusiastic, which will be noted by all the people you will come across. Contacts with friends and people having high social positions are noticeably activated. Thanks to them, you will solve many problems and strengthen your positions.

Relations with colleagues from other cities and countries are not bad; a successful business trip is possible.

Recent problems can emerge again in early February, but later, they will be resolved, one way or another.

February is very good for finding new friends and business partners. It can happen on a trip or in a circle of people who come from far away. In any case, new friends will be useful and communicating with them will make your life better.

Money. Your financial situation will improve, but it can't be called quite stable. As before, the stars strongly advise you to keep your business under control, make no promises and not vouch for anyone.

Also, be attentive to your friends and high-positioned patrons; if you use their services, negotiate the terms at the very beginning. This will save you from many problems both now and in the future.

Love. Family. There is a noticeable revival in your romantic life. February promises to the unmarried people and those disappointed in their previous relationships new acquaintances that will expand the communication circle. You can meet a new friend, and your relations can, with time, become quite special for you.

In one case, this will happen on a trip or in a circle of people who come from far away, in another - at school or in the circle of your former schoolmates.

The family relations are unstable or somewhat uncertain. There is a pause after the recent shakeups, but maybe it's just a calm before the storm?

Uranus will soon move to the sky sector responsible for family life and its foundations, which already happened in the summer of 2018. Remember this period - it can happen again, though in a more acute form.

Health. In February, you are healthy, active and energetic. But be careful on February 1 through 3 when traveling or driving. The probability of injuries and emergencies is high enough.

pisces

Now life gives you numerous chances to establish yourself in the best way possible. But you need to get ready, and this is what February is for.

Job. Career. In February, you can rely completely on your entourage. Your friends and like-minded people will be there, and their influence on your business will be absolutely positive. Now you must be able to work in a team, as well as work out some organizational matters as it's not so easy to put together the differing interests of those who support you.

The employee can strengthen his/her position at a new, recently obtained working place. Those who are only planning this, can get the necessary support and reach their goal within the next month.

The stars urge all the capable representatives of this sign to be active and move forward steadily - your time has come!

Towards the end of the month, contacts with colleagues from other cities or countries will be activated, a business trip or preparation for it is possible.

Money. Your financial situation as a whole is stable, there is an obvious tendency to improve it. Money can come from various sources. In addition to your own earnings, you can expect that your loved ones will support you.

The estimated dates for receiving the most substantial amounts are February 2, 9, 10, 18, 19, 26, 27. Large expenses are expected at the very beginning of the month - February 1, 2. On those days, money losses and theft are also possible. This should be taken into account by all representatives of this sign, especially those whose work is related to finance.

Love. Family. In February, despite working hard, you will be able to spend time with your loved ones. The spouses and the lovers can spend a few days together far from home. The relationships are even and harmonious. Perhaps your loved one will become more attentive to and even more dependent on you.

If your extremely active social life causes a loved one's jealousy, tell him/her how busy you are, but be more attentive. This will help you avoid numerous problems both now and later.

Health. In general, your energy potential is high enough, but lethargy, fatigue and a desire for rest are possible from time to time. Especially significant in this regard are the days of New Moon - February 3, 4, 5, when your energy potential will be at a zero point. Take care of your body on those days and avoid all kinds of excesses.

MARCH

ARIES

In March, you should stop, look back and analyze the issues
that were put off "till later."

Job. Career. For you, March will be a difficult month. In fact, this month traditionally brings many problems, and this time won't be an exception.

In the best-case scenario, the business will, for different reasons, slow down, while at worst, intrigues, obvious hostility, bad rumors and gossip are possible. You should sort it out and make the necessary conclusions. Most likely, this situation has been maturing for a long time and now it has its ugliest form. But it's not bad at all: if you face the problem and understand it, you can take the necessary measures and resolve it quickly.

Relations with your colleagues from other cities or countries will be very complicated. This should be taken into account by those whose activity depends on it. It is possible that your faraway partners will show their worst qualities again and the collaboration will hang in complete uncertainty...

Another option is that there will be legal problems or you will have to face a strange, incomprehensible behavior of the inspecting authorities from another country. In any case, cover your bases and watch your entourage. There are many people who envy you, and this time they can show themselves in all their "glory"!

Looking ahead, it's possible to say that the situation will only be partially resolved in April, but some complex issues will have to be dealt with more than once.

Money. Difficulties in business will not affect your finances too much. Money will be arriving in the planned quantities, and the largest amounts can be expected on March 1, 2, 11, 12, 17, 20, 28, 29.

Love. Family. In personal life, problems are also possible. Both the lovers and the spouses will have misunderstandings and quarrels in the last ten days of March. You may have to learn an unpleasant secret about a person close to you, or he/she will learn something about you. Beware of all kinds of intrigue and don't tell your secrets anyone. Be as prudent as possible.

Some representatives of your sign will have problems with relatives, though not theirs, but rather some of the spouse's. In this case, remember that now you are quite vulnerable, and try to behave diplomatically.

Health. Those who won't have professional and personal misfortunes can have health problems. Be especially careful during the New Moon days on March 5 through 7 - this period will be difficult for you in all aspects. The drivers and the travelers should be more careful, since accidents and various complications are possible.

In March, trips are not recommended, so please abstain from all kinds of traveling.

TAURUS

In March, you will have to decide who is your friend and who is your enemy, as well as who is neither friend nor enemy.

Job. Career. In March, you may see that not everyone in your entourage shares your ideas and views. More than that, your friends and like-minded people can start fighting on either financial or common property grounds. It's hardly possible to say that you are absolutely right as you are to blame in some cases, like your opponents in others. The truth is somewhere in between, and if you understand this, it will be much easier for you to find a solution.

There is also a possibility of serious disagreements related to debt obligations, taxes as well as credits taken in the past. If this is the case, you will have to negotiate, sign and redo the documents, and face opposition from official structures. The solution will be found not in March, but later - perhaps by mid April.

And if the circumstances made the situation tough for you and the audits are unbearable, ask experienced lawyers to help you - this will be the best thing you can do.

In a less stressful variant, you will have to make investments to expand your business, and the expenses will be greater than expected.

Relations with colleagues from other cities or countries are going on well provided that those are time-tested ties. In some cases, it is those contacts that will help you find a solution in the complicated situation created by your entourage.

Money. In this kind of business, financial problems are inevitable. Money is spent almost constantly, and, towards the end of March, your wallet will be much emptier than before. In one case, the reason is your business, in another, your personal life.

Love. Family. In your personal life, various trends are possible. For example, the married people are still busy arranging their homes and investing a lot of money in those projects.

There is a chance of problems with friends, difficulties paying off the debts, and other financial issues. If you experience such problems, you will need help from your relatives, including your spouse's relatives or your loved ones living in another city or country.

For people in love, this month is also difficult. For different reasons, relationships can become much worse. In one case, the reason will be business problems, while in the other, your entourage interfering in your love affairs.

General advice for those in love: don't pay attention to rumors and gossip, and do your best to protect your love from prying eyes!

Health. In March, your energy potential is high enough, but this month's general atmosphere of nervousness may result in your feeling tired and "de-energized" by the end of the month. Remember about this and take time to rest and sleep, even if you are very busy. This will help you avoid many problems both now and in the future.

GEMINI

In March, you are very active and ambitious. It's OK, but you should try to make sure that your ambitions don't spoil your relations with others.

Job. Career. It is possible that you will spend the whole month fighting. The entrepreneurs and managers of all levels can have conflicts with their business partners. In one case, it will be about revising the general business objectives, while in another - about dividing the business.

The confrontation will be serious, and you will have to make an effort to defend your position. Looking ahead, it's possible to say that the problem will hardly be solved this month; most likely, it will happen, in the best-case scenario, in April.

The stars recommend you not to hurry and worry. It is very important to act competently and accurately, so don't react to provocations, keep your emotions, and defend your positions step by step. There is no need to make big concessions, but try to reach a compromise acceptable for you.

The employee will have competitors, but he/she will be able to come to terms with the boss, although it will at first be difficult. You will only achieve clarity by the end of March or even in April. Perhaps you will have to ask your friends or high-positioned acquaintances to help you solve the problems.

Money. In March, you will have some serious financial conflicts. You will make a lot of effort to defend your finances from the encroachments of your greedy entourage, but the game is worth the candle. In the long run, you will achieve a more or less fair distribution, but, most likely, you will get less than expected. However, at this stage, it is an achievement anyway, so go ahead!

Love. Family. It is not excluded that this month, business interests and personal relations will come into conflict. Professionally active representatives of this sign won't have time for love and romance in March, which you should explain politely and tactfully to your loved one in order to avoid misunderstandings.

Problems with the partner's family are also possible, which will affect the relationship. There can be various reasons, but you must hope that, in the long run, love will overcome all the barriers. Perhaps this is your case.

Health. This month, Mercury, your governor, goes backwards, which means that you will be restless, fussy and nervous. You can neutralize all this by having enough sleep and spending more time out of town. As the saying goes, "Work hard, but play harder."

CANCER

For you, March events can have long-term consequences,
that's why it is necessary to act cautiously and thoughtfully.
As the saying goes, "Patience always pays off."

Job. Career. The main thing in March is to clarify your relations with the colleagues from other cities and countries. The entrepreneurs and managers of all levels will face very serious processes that have long been developing in the relations with your remote business partners. Now you can't ignore this problem, because it will face you in full growth.

One of the options is that productive work can be hampered by certain legal issues. Another one is the inconsistent and, perhaps, even dishonest behavior of your business partners living in a different city or country. It won't be possible to find a quick solution, and, most likely, clarity will only be achieved in April.

The best thing you can do in March is to resort to the help of your old friends, who don't give advice not asked for, but are always ready to help. And if there are people in your entourage who possess power and influence, ask them to help you - it will also work well.

This advice is also relevant for those who have long-standing legal problems or have to deal with auditors.

Money. Professional problems will affect your finances: you will have much less money. But you won't be penniless and can expect some money flow in late March as well as in April.

Love. Family. This month, reviving old relationships will be important for you. You can also meet with old acquaintances and friends you have not seen for a long time. Resuming a previous romantic relationship is also possible.

The spouses who quarrelled earlier can, for various reasons, come to terms and will perhaps begin truce talks. Don't miss your chance even if the truce is not going to last long! Your loved one's support in this difficult period can seriously improve your positions in all areas.

The influence of the relatives on the family relationship will be rather positive, especially if they don't talk too much and try to be more polite.

Trips scheduled for March will be successful, if you are going to the places you know very well. Otherwise, you can't avoid disappointment and all kinds of problems.

Be attentive when dealing with new people you come across - they won't be who they say they are, but it will only become clear 3 months later.

Health. This month, your health is not very stable, so try to get enough sleep, and eat by the clock.

Also, be attentive when traveling and driving.

LEO

March will mean a rigid frame for you. Usually, you move to your goal steadily, but now the stars recommend you to stop and not allow anyone to rush you.

Job. Career. March is not at all simple for professional matters. Positive and negative effects of the Cosmos are distributed equally, so you need to be able to find the best solutions in all situations you find yourself in.

There is a chance of difficult negotiations related to finance, as well as working with banks, credits, or just paying old debts off.

The entrepreneurs and managers will resume working on an old project, involving their "old", reliable colleagues.

The employee can count on an offer from his/her former employer. Please consider it well and discuss the conditions.

For many representatives of your sign, some old projects will get a new life, though on a solid and up-to-date basis.

Money. You will have financial problems this month. Many of you will have to pay off your old debts, try to find additional funds for themselves or for their loved ones.

The stars recommend those who work in the sphere of finance to check the documents carefully in order to avoid errors.

At the same time, you won't be penniless as decent amounts of money will be hitting your account from time to time, so by the end of the month you will keep financial balance.

Love. Family. You will face some difficulties in your personal life. The spouses are concerned about their children's problems, which can result in large financial expenses.

Expenses related to house renovation are also quite likely.

The lovers will have conflicts related to differing life outlooks or to financial issues. Perhaps, you will find your loved one's claims excessive and, most likely, you will be right.

Health. This month, your energy potential is low and this will be especially obvious in New Moon - March 5-7. Try to spend this time calmly and remember that if you fall ill in New Moon, it can last very long.

VIRGO

There is a lot of confusion in your ranks now. You should define your main objectives and try not to kill two birds with one stone as both may fly away.

Job. Career. In March, there is a danger of getting into some kind of dependence on your business partners. The latter can behave far from ideally – not fulfill their obligations, disregard your calls and refuse answering your letters, or even deceive you on numerous important business issues. This can last throughout the whole month and will only be resolved in April.

A positive tendency in March can be developing contacts with your colleagues from other cities or countries. They can render you the necessary assistance, which will partially stabilize the situation. Trips scheduled for this month will be successful.

March is good for renewing old contacts. If you have a problem, you can contact an old friend. As to the new acquaintances you come across in March, treat them with a fair share of skepticism - most likely, they will be of no or little use.

The employee should take into account that March is not very good for communicating with the boss and official institutions. Patience, prudence and attention to the documents are your most important qualities; if you use them, you will avoid many troubles that are quite possible this month.

Money. In March, you will probably have financial problems, which is quite natural under the circumstances. This can last long, so save your money instead of wasting it.

Love. Family. Those who have no business problems will have difficulties in their personal life.

The married people can quarrel more than usual, the problem being some unresolved issues related to the renovation of their home. Your children's influence will somewhat mitigate the situation and smooth out the existing contradictions.

The lovers can have conflicts because of their parents or older relatives. If this is the case, be tactful and patient in order to reduce the number of tough issues.

The stars recommend both lovers and spouses to go on a joint trip to a familiar place.

March is good for renewing the old ties and visiting places well known to you, while new acquaintances and unfamiliar cities and countries will bring you disappointment.

Health. This month, your energy potential is low, so try to be less nervous and fussy. Remember that all diseases are caused by stress and worries, so behave accordingly.

LIBRA

In March, you will have to understand that there is no direct road to success, and there is a surprise behind every turn. It will not be easy to overcome this, but you don't seem to have another solution!

Job. Career. This month, most representatives of your sign will face a number of problems. The entrepreneurs and the managers will have to solve complex problems related to business partners from other cities or countries. Some of them will not fulfill their obligations, play their own game and hamper your business in every possible way. But there is a chance that they will prefer cooperation to confrontation and act accordingly.

Besides, many will face some confusion among their subordinates, who will start a complex intrigue, or whose unprofessional activity will nullify an important undertaking. Negligence and fraud are also possible.

At the same time, business related to some large property, maybe land or real estate, is going on well.

The employee can face a big intrigue, and he/she is recommended not to take anyone's side. You run a risk of letting yourself down and being the one to blame.

Those who have legal problems are recommended to ask a good specialist for help, because the problems may be more difficult than expected.

Money. Despite the difficult business situation, no money problems will occur in March. It will be arriving regularly, and the largest amounts can be expected on March 15, 16, 23-25.

Love. Family. In your personal life, the main achievement can be solving real estate issues. The friendly spouses can start serious repair and overcome the obstacles together. A smaller event is purchasing furniture and other items that make your everyday life better.

The divorcing couples can face problems related to dividing the real estate property.

In both cases, all kinds of delays are inevitable this month, which you should take into account in advance.

Relations with your relatives will become somewhat worse, but everything will go back to normal next month. You will have no reason to quarrel with your relatives, the more so that they are not planning anything bad.

Health. In March, your energy potential is low, so spend time on vacation, best of all at a sanatorium not far from your home. Long-distance trips are not recommended in March as they are likely not to be up to your expectations.

The car drivers should be more careful when driving a car as there is a high probability of accidents, tickets and other unpleasant events.

SCORPIO

This month, love is at stake as well as your personal relations in general. Make a decision by yourself and don't let anyone rush you!

Job. Career. Although the main March events can have a personal character, you can also do something important in your business.

This month, the main achievement is resuming relations with your colleagues from other cities or countries. Most likely, those are old, time-tested ties, which will help you start a new business or resume the "old" one, though on a more up-to-date basis.

Not everything will go on smoothly in this area. Financial disagreements are possible, and they will be resolved not earlier than in April. But all of them will be related to work, and, in general, the planned collaboration can be called positive.

It's possible that relatives will take part in your undertakings and influence your projects in a very favorable way.

All professionally active representatives of this sign are advised to check the documents carefully, avoid hurrying and making fuss. Don't rush to sign important contracts. This must be done not earlier than in April.

Money. March is a month of large expenses, most of which are related to the family or romantic affairs. As they say, "everyone has one's own headache."

Love. Family. This month, the sphere of personal relations can become uncontrollable and make you feel anxious. For example, the lovers may have serious conflicts because they have different visions of the future of their relationship, even different systems of values.

Another option is having serious financial problems. If you believe that your loved one is going to "ruin you", remember that this will be resolved quickly.

If you are male, simply pamper your loved one, and do it sincerely, without reproaching her. In the long run, everything will be OK.

The parents will have problems with their children, and a large portion of the family budget will be spent to resolve those problems.

In March, older relatives will make a positive influence on all the difficult situations. Address the elders whenever you face a problem.

If you plan a trip, choose a well-known place, because visiting unfamiliar cities or countries can disappoint you.

Health. This month, you are healthy, energetic and enterprising, and these qualities will help you solve all your problems.

SAGITTARIUS

In March, your interests may, for different reasons, differ from what others want. Stick to the rules and remember that you are not always right.

Job. Career. This month is not very good for professional undertakings. The best thing you can do is to analyze your plans and make the required corrections.

The entrepreneurs and the managers are advised to check their business and think of recruiting new staff. Don't involve new people this month. It would be a great idea to make a plan for the future and think about who you really need.

Almost all of March, Mercury will be moving backwards, which means that this month acquaintances will bring you no benefit. But if colleagues from the past appear, their proposals should be taken into account.

The employee is recommended to be modest; if he/she is going to communicate with the boss, ask no questions, but, rather, offer solutions.

All representatives of your sign should take into account that this month, you will have to strain yourself to do things overcoming the resistance of circumstances as well as your own reluctance to act. If this happens to you, consider having a rest or spending the weekend out of town.

Money. In March, your financial situation is relatively stable, but you should not expect any serious success. Certain amounts of money can be expected on March 10-12, 19-21, 28, 29.

Expenses are inevitable, and, as the astrologer believes, most of them will be related to the home, children and family in general.

Love. Family. In March, many representatives of your sign will pay a lot of attention to their personal and family affairs. Quite different situations are possible.

Even in the most friendly families, the atmosphere is far from ideal. In one case, this is caused by the changes in the lifestyle, renovation or unexpected arrival of guests.

The unfriendly spouses can have a serious conflict, which may result in separation or divorce.

Think twice before starting all this. If you decide to go on, be consistent, but remember that there will be no way back.

And if you have a new love affair, think well if you can live together and whether your love story is going to have continuation. Is it a good idea to destroy what you have?

Health. This month, your energy potential is low, there is a chance of lethargy, fatigue, lack of desire to do anything at all.

In this case, remember about the benefits of morning exercises and walking as well as a balanced diet. Weight gain is possible, so please take care!

CAPRICORN

Remember that your entourage are people of many moods. Also, this month, the proverb "Speech is silver, silence is golden" will be quite relevant.

Job. Career. In March, you should not make important decisions or promises.

The entrepreneurs and the managers must remember that someone can, by chance or intentionally, interfere with their plans or lead them astray.

Those who have contacts with colleagues from other cities or countries will face difficulties again. The faraway business partners can act differently than expected: they can go back on their word, make delays, or refuse to collaborate. Another option is that circumstances may affect your joint business, which will hardly be overcome this month.

Business trips scheduled for this month may fail, and if there is no emergency, it would be a good idea to cancel them.

The employee should be more attentive: some team members are not friendly at all, someone will let you down at the first opportunity.

All representatives of your sign should remember that this month's news may be false and should be checked twice. Also, beware of gossip and intrigue.

There is something else. Don't let anyone else do your job. It can be done in other months, but not now!

Keep all processes under control – you are the only person who will be able to cope with all the complex situations of this month, including the unexpected audits.

Money. Your business problems won't affect the finances, whose amount will, most likely, not decrease. Venus is in the financial sector of your sky, which means that your money will be OK.

Love. Family. In your personal life, March can make you face difficult tasks, and you will need to exert maximum effort to solve them.

In many families, relations with relatives will become much more complicated. In one case, they will be playing their own game and lead you astray; in another, one of your relatives may fall ill or have other problems, so your help and support will be needed.

The lovers should beware of rumors, intrigues and the possibility of their secrets being revealed unexpectedly.

Health. Those who are lucky enough to avoid professional and personal difficulties may have health problems. The stars strongly advise you to be careful on trips and when driving, due to a high probability of accidents in March.

AQUARIUS

It's important to have no illusions this month. Facing the world with your eyes open is not fun, but it's better to see it as it is. Stay focused - this will let you avoid a lot of problems both now and in the future.

Job. Career. In March, you should not take on serious business or make important acquaintances. You can make numerous mistakes assessing people and events. Now it would be better to put things in order, especially those that are related to finance.

There is a chance of disagreements with your friends or some high-positioned people about money or debt obligations. It is also possible that you will have to resolve problems related to real estate; all financial disputes will have something to do with this circumstance.

The entrepreneurs and managers are likely to negotiate moving to another office and buying land, but only preliminary steps are possible this month, while the final decision will be made not earlier than in May.

Money. You will focus on financial issues for most of March.

The stars warn you: this month's proverb "Money likes to be counted" will be quite relevant: if you follow it, you can avoid a lot of troubles both now and in the future.

Those whose job is related to finances should be especially cautious. They should remember that mistakes are highly probable in March and they can be very costly.

Love. Family. This month, Uranus, your governor, is moving to the sky sector which is responsible for the home, family and relations with relatives, and will stay there for 7 years.

Uranus is an innovative planet, even a revolutionary one, so there can be serious changes in all areas of your life.

Many representatives of your sign will intend to move to a new house/apartment. In some cases, this may happen within the next 3-4 months.

Your family relations will also develop in a different way: all unnecessary things will go away gradually, but everything related to love and life will stay. This can be applied both to the lovers and to the spouses.

By the end of the month, relations between both will get worse, but these are just insignificant quarrels, there is nothing serious about them.

Health. In March, your energy potential is low, lethargy, fatigue, mood swings are highly possible. If all this happens to you, try to be active, go out of town as often as possible, and remember that no troubles "are here to stay", so everything will be much better next month.

pisces

In March, you are recommended to avoid rushing and fussing. The proverb "Measure twice, cut once" will be surprisingly appropriate this time!

Job. Career. This month will be full of contradictions. You have big plans, but it's necessary to get ready for tackling the tasks and not lose sight of the small things. This is what March is for.

You will have good relations with the colleagues from other cities or countries. Old friends will be helping you and if you use their abilities correctly, you will succeed in advancing your business.

Many can expect starting a business in another city or another country; in some cases, you will have to relocate.

The situation will be fully clarified next month; presently, you should finalize your projects, make necessary corrections, and take your time preparing a solid foundation for the future business.

The employee is recommended to do his/her job diligently and, if possible, not argue with the boss. And if it is a matter of a new job, think twice about it. It would be a good idea to put the final decision off till April.

Money. Your financial situation will improve by the end of the month, and this trend will continue in April. The estimated dates for receiving the largest amounts of money are March 25-27.

Love. Family. Serious changes are possible in your personal life. In many families, relations with relatives living in a different city or country will become more active; over time, this may result in relocation.

The lovers can also get ready for moving, especially if your loved one lives far away. In one case, this will happen in the next three months, while in another, in different periods of 2019.

Health. This is a month of fuss and unrest, so it's possible that in late March you won't be quite cheerful and confident. The stars advise you not to make unnecessary moves, have a rest and sleep more.

APRIL

ARIES

April will teach you a lot - first of all that everything is equally important.

Job. Career. Contacts with colleagues from other cities or countries are as important as before. Compared to the previous month, those contacts will be improved significantly, but the situation won't be quite stable.

There is a chance of complications caused by subjective and objective reasons. The former include malevolence of your hidden and overt enemies as well as the sluggishness of your employees.

Another option is that your expectations may conflict with the abilities of your partners, while their wishes won't be up to your expectations. So analyze all the options in advance, and take measures. This will let you avoid numerous misunderstandings, both at present and in the future.

The employee is recommended to be more attentive to his/her colleagues and make intrigues impossible. If you are offered a new job, it would be a good idea to review carefully its conditions and pay attention to all the details before signing the contract. This advice is important for all representatives of your sign, no matter what kind of job they have.

Money. Preparations you have long been engaged in will bring you a good income.

You can expect it in late April or in the first half of May. You can get some money on April 7, 8, 16, 17, 24-26.

Love. Family. No serious changes will happen in your personal life. It's possible that you will be so overwhelmed with your job that love and family will go to the background. However, a loved one is ready to help you and will do it effectively and politely.

Relations with your loved ones are still far from ideal. A serious conflict is likely, in which almost all members of your family will be involved. You can hardly neutralize the situation, so be ready for acting as an arbiter for your conflicting relatives.

Health. In April, your energy potential is high enough, but the stars strongly advise you to be more careful on trips and while driving.

TAURUS

This month, the best thing you can do is to finalize the work started earlier and correct the mistakes. The good news is that the mistakes will be quite obvious and easy to correct.

Job. Career. You still have financial problems. Many representatives of your sign will conduct difficult negotiations with a friend or with people occupying a high social position. Perhaps, it will again be about money, debts or other financial issues. Please remember that, in some cases, you will need the help of a good lawyer to resolve them.

Relations with colleagues from other cities or countries are going on well. Your old friends will help you in this aspect and, probably, they will support you in resolving numerous April's problematic issues.

If you plan to relocate or start a business in another city or country, you just can't do without the old ties.

The employee looking for another application to his/her talents can probe the ground and have a series of important business meetings. There won't be an immediate result, but it is better than nothing.

Money. In April, your financial situation may not be very stable. The stars recommend you to avoid unnecessary spending and be reasonable in everything that concerns money and other material values.

In April, your expenses will be related not only to business, but to personal life as well.

Love. Family. There are still problems in your family life. A lot of money will be required to tackle serious housing issues. But if you analyze your expenses, you will certainly find a way to make big savings. If problems arise, you can ask your older relatives to help you, and even if their help is not substantial, it is better than nothing. In some cases, real estate operations can be performed in another city or country and have something to do with a planned relocation.

Relationships between the lovers are rather complicated; a cooling or a quarrel are possible.

This month, you are very vulnerable, that's why you should be more modest and not hurt the feelings of your loved ones. This will do good to everyone.

Health. In April, your energy potential is low, so, despite the problems and urgent matters, find time to relax. This will let you have more pleasant minutes and fewer unpleasant ones.

GEMINI

You are both active and conflicting throughout the month. It's OK, but try to strive for really important goals. As you know, the eagle doesn't catch flies.

Job. Career. Your professional affairs acquire certainty and clarity, but there is something you just can't be happy with. On the one hand, those are financial issues, on the other – the attitude of your business partners, who are trying to claim all the achievements. These problems will be growing gradually throughout the month and, towards its end, enough will be enough. If this happens to you, please mind that your partners still have a stronger position, so, before acting, you should plan your own actions very well.

However, the situation is not so bad, there are bright moments, too. In particular, you will do a lot to improve your business, settle some financial issues, as well as make useful acquaintances.

As to the professional affairs, the best time is the first and second tenday periods of April. During this time, the employee can strengthen his/her positions and improve relations with the boss, while the self-employed will discover new opportunities and find new business partners.

Money. April financial situation is uneven. On the one hand, it seems that you get more money. On the other hand, the expenses increase, too.

In one case, they are related to the business partners, while in the other – to your loved ones.

Love. Family. This month, many representatives of your sign will be more busy working and socializing, so there will be too little time left for personal life.

For various reasons, however, there are problems in this area. There will be no open conflicts, but in late April or early May, the growing irritation can lead to a serious conflict, and you are the most likely initiator. Think about it at leisure. These relationships are important for you, so would it be a good idea to destroy them? This advice is equally relevant for the "new" spouses and for the lovers.

Health. This month, you are energetic, quite healthy, but very conflictful and irritable. Your main task is to achieve inner balance and harmony. To some of you, meditation and yoga will do good, while others would prefer lying on a sofa and reading a book.

CANCER

In April, the sky will clear up for you, which mainly refers to your job. As to your personal life, everything will be quite the other way about.

Job. Career. This month, doing things will be easy for you, no matter what you do. Use the star position and take on the new project boldly!

The complicated relations with the colleagues from other cities or countries will be settled in some way. It is possible that you will be assisted by your old friends or some of your business partners. Trips scheduled for April will be successful.

At the same time, the old problem can't be considered fully settled. You will have to face it many times in the future, but as long as you can clarify and improve the situation, do it please.

Your business is doing much better, but April will bring you some problems, too. For example, you will have conflicts with some of your business partners. You faced that in the past, too, that's why this situation is nothing new for you and you understand what you should do about it.

Those who have legal problems can improve their standing, but you should not relax completely as the final solution is still far away.

The employee will have better relations with his/her boss; there is a chance of getting a higher position or a higher salary.

Those who look for a chance to apply their talents in a different way can count on this month and go ahead and tackle new challenges.

Money. Your financial situation will improve, which may be a natural result of the improvement in your business. The estimated dates for receiving the most serious amounts are April 4-6, 13-15, 21, 22.

Love. Family. The situation in your personal life is not simple again. The still existing conflict with your ex began long ago, and you have no idea what you can do about it.

Representatives of your sign cling to the past and continue the lifeless and loveless relationship... It's not good to just wait and see, one of you has to take the plunge. This, of course, refers to those who have been stressed for many years now.

However, the stable couples can also feel intercooling. In this case, a trip is recommended, it will refresh your thoughts and feelings.

Health. In April, you are energetic, active and quite healthy. However, those who have chronic diseases are recommended to monitor their state: the illness that seemed to have retreated can return in 4 or 6 weeks, so don't stop the medical treatment.

LEO

This month, you will have a chance to try something new, but, so far, it's just a chance. You need time and effort to turn the chance into reality!

Job. Career. There are new undertakings and projects that can raise your business to a new level. There is a possibility that, at some point, they will conflict with what you are doing right now, but this will be a temporary situation. Some time later, you will combine them and benefit from that.

Relations with the partners from other cities or countries are going on well, but in mid April, some difficulties are possible, which, however, will be resolved quickly.

The stars recommend the bosses and the entrepreneurs to pay more attention to their subordinates as the latter can be not flexible enough as well slow and incompetent. Perhaps it's time to think about shuffling the team or changing some of its members.

The employee can negotiate a new job or, a bit later, get an interesting offer.

Money. Your financial situation is stable, your business partners can provide a good support to you, there is a chance of getting sponsorship, having credits and paying the old debts off. Those who have nothing to do with business can count on the help from their loved ones.

There will also be substantial expenses, related mainly to your children and loved ones as well as to your family's needs.

Love. Family. In personal life, you can expect very pleasant events. You can have addition to the family – new children and grandchildren.

As to the lovers, April won't be an easy month. There is a growing mutual dissatisfaction, which can result in a serious conflict. The last week of

April and the last ten days of May are the most problematic periods as the probability of a quarrel is rather high. It's hard to foresee what will happen in each particular case, but there is a cause for concern.

A trip would be a good solution: a week spent far from home will let you look at many things at a different angle, and what used to irritate you may seem not important at all.

Health. In April, your energy potential is high enough, but those who have long-standing problems with the spine and the body's motor system should pay more attention to their health, because in mid April, complications are quite possible.

In the same period, the drivers are recommended to drive very carefully.

VIRGO

For you, April is a traditionally difficult month. There won't be any exclusion this time: positive influences of the stars can interchange in bizarre way with negative ones, so you will have to be flexible enough and maneuver so as not to miss the positive influences and avoid the negative ones.

Job. Career. It's a time of change and serious reorganization in your business. Besides, you will have to deal with the colleagues who, for various reasons, won't accept your proposals and will be quite outspoken about it. It's very important for you to be realistic when assessing your capabilities and not to give unrealistic promises.

At the same time, your business requires changes, and they will certainly happen. There is a chance of real estate operations, moving, purchasing, renting or selling the industrial premises.

The employee can also face organizational changes, which may result in dismissal. If all this happens to you, ask your loved ones to help you as there is no one else who can really support you.

Money. Financial problems are likely with this state of the arts in business. Serious expenses are expected; some of you will spend money for their business matters, while others will have to deal with family needs and the needs of their loved ones.

Love. Family. In your personal life, everything is OK. This month, the stars even advise you to consider your loved ones' opinion when taking important decisions as those people are your real support. Your children will require a lot of attention. It is possible that their needs will take most of the family budget.

For those in love, April is not very successful. You can be too irritable and stubborn. On the other hand, you partner will behave in a similar way.

Your feelings, thoughts and even words can be separated by an invisible though almost insurmountable barrier, and this won't bring you anything good.

Think twice before speaking and making judgments. Don't say what you can't unsay. These recommendations are especially important in the third tenday period of the month, when the probability of conflicts is rather high.

Health. In April, your energy potential is not high, so take care of yourself and be reasonable. Weak and elderly people should be especially cautious.

LIBRA

In April, the sky above you will clear up and the problems that seemed very hard and even unresolvable will be solved at last. Yes, it won't be easy, but you are going the right way, which means that the victory is close!

Job. Career. Throughout the month, you will probably be busy communicating with your business partners, colleagues and subordinates. Some of them still behave not as expected. There is a chance of conflicts related to large property, such as real estate, land, or disputed, not divided lots. Working in this direction will require much time, but keep putting one foot in front of the other.

Relations with the colleagues from other cities or countries won't be stable, there will be some problems on the way to complete understanding, and they will require analysis and careful work.

Towards the end of the month, there will be a conflict among your foreign colleagues, and you will have to be engaged in reconciling the two hostile parties.

Besides, the entrepreneurs of all ranks should look attentively at their subordinates, while the employees must be careful about the behavior of their colleagues.

In both cases, there is a possibility of direct or indirect fraud, intrigues, unwillingness to consider the circumstances, laziness and mistakes.

There is a lot of work ahead, so roll your sleeves up and act!

Money. You will have many problems of a professional nature, but you will have enough money. It will be coming as before and the amount will be the same. April expenses will also be predictable and reasonable.

Love. Family. Those for whom their private life is a priority, can face another conflict with their partner, and painful real-estate issues will appear on the agenda again. But this only refers to the couples having a long history of mutual claims and grievances.

The friendly spouses will work together to resolve complex household and financial issues, using patience, wisdom and undying love.

In the first half of the month, relations with the loved ones are quite harmonious. However, towards the end of April as well as in May, misunderstandings and quarrels are possible among the relatives. You will probably be involved, though in the honorary role of arbitrator.

You should get ready for the trips scheduled for April. The best time for traveling is the last tenday period of the month.

Health. In April, your energy potential is low, so it would be a good idea to spend the whole weekend or at least a few hours out of town.

Throughout April, and, especially, in its third tenday period, the drivers are advised to be more careful while driving a car.

SCORPIO

In April, you should be very attentive to details and all kinds of small things, both in professional matters and romantic relationships.

Job. Career. In April, you can be overwhelmed with important current issues. To avoid being drowned in this stream, the stars recommend you to structure your activities and set priorities on time.

Contacts with colleagues from other cities or countries are going on well. There will be minor problems in the middle of the month, but you will overcome them quickly.

You will renew your old contacts and, probably, meet with your former business partners residing in other cities or countries. Besides, you will have collaboration opportunities with someone new to you; a little later, those opportunities will become a reality.

The employee will be get additional responsibilities, quite beneficial for him/her.

Money. In terms of finance, this month can be uneven. You will have more money, but you expenses will grow, too. Most likely, their main part will be related to your romantic relationship or your family.

At the same time, all representatives of your sign must take into account that Mars, a very aggressive planet, will threaten your financial stability in April and in May. So try not to enter into questionable deals. Also, you should not risk your own money or the money or other valuables entrusted to you. There is a high probability of unexpected losses, which should be taken into account by all representatives of your sign and especially by those who work with money, such as accountants, brokers, bank employees and others.

Love. Family. This month is very tough for romantic relationships. For example, you want to turn the old friendship into something more significant. What should you do? How can you convince the one you love that love is still alive after so many months and even years? To wait and see doesn't seem to be a good idea, you must take the plunge. And if you are serious about it, you will make the decisive step.

But mind that now you may be separated by many things, such as different views, different systems of values, and even financial disagreements...

The married people will have problems with their children, but, most likely, those are just expenses for the needs of the younger generation.

Health. This month, your energy potential is not high. Please try to get enough sleep and eat by the clock.

In mid April, the stars advise the drivers to be more careful while driving as there is a very high probability of car accidents.

SAGITTARIUS

You are very lucky and will be able to solve many problems. Optimism and confidence, your true assistants, will accompany you throughout April.

Job. Career. During most of the month, you will be quite eager to do your best to defend your ideas and principles. If this is the case, here is the advice: find convincing arguments and use a simple and comprehensible way of explaining them.

Relations with some of your business partners are not very harmonious; a serious conflict is probable towards the end of April. Its possible reasons are ambitions on both parts, or financial claims.

You can also face problems related to some disputed real estate. But in general, this month is not bad for you at all: you can have new acquaintances as well as new ideas having good implementation perspectives.

Money. In terms of finance, April will probably be uneven.

Your income is small, while the expenses are growing, and their main part is related to the needs of your children or loved ones. You can have some income thanks to various real estate operations, such as, for example, renting.

Love. Family. Love affairs never develop smoothly. This time, too, you will have conflicts, heartbreaking scenes, and talks about inevitable parting. But the fact is that both of you treasure your relationships, and it would be a bad idea to lose them due to ridiculous ambitions. Understanding this will open up the road to reconciliation!

Those who have it both ways can face a very big problem in April, when they have to maneuver trying not to fall between the two chairs. This problem, which is quite probable in late April or in the first tenday period of May, can destroy the romantic tale for a long time or perhaps even forever.

Health. In April, you will have enough energy for everything. The stars only advise you to use it constructively.

CAPRICORN

In April, patience and stubbornness can be your business card. Although some people won't like this, you will definitely achieve your goals.

Job. Career. This month, you can tackle important organizational matters.

You will go on with real estate operations; in some cases, they will take place in another city or country.

Those who dream of launching a business somewhere faraway, can make a decisive step in April and achieve a lot.

At the same time, the stars recommend you to be careful: audit authorities may show interest to your activity. Another possibility is that the law will suddenly block your road and you will have to look for a detour. But you will certainly reach the goal.

The entrepreneurs and the managers are recommended to be attentive to some of the employees, whose excessive independence annoys them and can harm the business.

For most of the employees, April is not very good. You should not come up with important initiatives, contact your boss or criticize your colleagues. Instead, you are highly recommended to take a vacation and travel far away for a week or two.

And remember that most of your problems will occur in late April and early May.

Money. The financial sphere is rather calm, without significant successes or failures.

Love. Family. In April, many representatives of your sign will come across home and family issues.

There will be more changes in your everyday life; in one case, it is a major renovation, in another - acquisition of a new house/apartment. Acquisition of property in another city or country is possible.

In many families, relations are, for various reasons, far from ideal. Conflicts will become permanent and, most likely, it will be, to a large extent, your fault. Being irritable and picky is not good for a relationship, and if you have long been like that, you can definitely expect a similar reaction from your partner. In this case, even the stars can't give you any reasonable advice, because if you once chose this slippery road, you can hardly make a turn.

Health. This month, your energy potential is not high. Frequent lethargy and fatigue are possible. The best cure is traveling out of town and exercising or resting on the beach.

AQUARIUS

It's time for a change and moving forward. It's time to clear up the way to the future!

Job. Career. In April, last month problems will be partly solved. Those are complex financial issues, in which your friends or high-position people can be involved. Difficult negotiations can result in an acceptable compromise. But you should not relax, because the problems that seemed to be solved can arise again in the nearest future.

Relations with your colleagues from other cities or countries will not be even. There is a chance of trips, meetings with friends and people of high social standing.

In mid April, however, some obstacles will arise in relations with your foreign business partners or those located in other cities. For example, your plans can be hampered by law, an unexpected change in the international situation, or another force majeure event.

However, you will find solutions and, in the long run, everything will be OK.

The employee will get additional assignments, maybe requiring a business trip.

Money. Your financial situation is complicated, or, rather, contradictory. On the one hand, you get more and more money from official and unofficial sources. On the other hand, you have significant business- and family-related expenses.

But don't worry: you will keep a positive balance towards the end of April.

Love. Family. There are many changes in your personal life. You have relocation plans, but they will remain just plans for the next 18 months.

In one case, it's moving to a new house/apartment, in another – relocating to another city or country.

Relationships between the lovers are unstable and a big quarrel is likely. Late April and early May are especially dangerous in this regard; in that period, mutual dissatisfaction will reach its peak. Perhaps the conflict will be related to the different views on the future of the relationship and different value systems. In the worst-case scenario, understanding will be hampered by money or other financial issues.

The parents may have problems with their children, which will result in large expenses.

Many representatives of your sign will have more active relations with their relatives, but not everything will be OK in this area. Old claims and grievances can keep hampering communication, and you won't be able to overcome this yet.

Health. In April, you are healthy, energetic and very communicative. Your energy potential is rather high, but the stars highly recommend you to be more careful when traveling and driving.

pisces

April is going to be rather successful in everything related to money and business. As to your personal life, the sky will be cloudy again.

Job. Career. In April, you will be disciplined, full of optimism and self-confidence, which will certainly influence positively everything you do. Your old friends or high-position people will render you support and help you resolve the past month problems as well as agree on new projects. Your colleagues from other cities or countries will be involved in some of them. Over time, this direction can be very much in demand.

The employee is also having a good period, but, at the same time, he/she should not be too self-confident or bother the boss. It will be better to address all the proposals to the boss's assistants, some of whom definitely like you and your ideas.

Money. The financial situation is stable, and there is an obvious trend for improvement. You will get rather a large amount of money in mid April. Besides, you can expect a certain amount on April 22-23.

Love. Family. In the family life, a serious improvement is possible. It can include a big renovation, changes in your everyday life, and even moving. The friendly couples will work together on those issues, but even they may have disagreements on some household-related problems. As to the quarrelling couples, painful topics can arise in April, related to real estate, and in many cases, divorce and division of common property will become a reality.

The singles will make sudden acquaintances and meet old friends or ex-partners. A new romance is possible as well as plans related to a trip. So you won't be bored, and that's very important!

Health. In April, Mercury and Venus will provide a good support to you, that's why you will stay healthy. You will face this month's challenges with your head held high!

MAY

ARIES

This month, you will have another chance, and you will definitely take advantage of it. Keep going!

Job. Career. Go ahead and, despite the holiday time, use the shiny May days to improve your business. Communication with the colleagues from other cities or countries is still important, this is the most interesting and important direction. You have already done much, but more is to be done. This road will be both successful and problematic for you.

Your efforts will improve the situation greatly, but the complex unsolved issues need to be analyzed and discussed.

Most of the conflicts will take place on May 4 through May 6, after which the situation will stabilizes. Much will depend on you and your ability to come to terms with your business partners. That's why you should keep the initiative.

The employee can get job offers from foreign companies, which may be rather interesting in the intellectual and financial aspects.

Money. In terms of finance, May is quite successful. You will be receiving money on a regular basis, both from official and unofficial sources. The good news is that you will not only increase your own income, but can also count on strengthening your loved ones' financial positions.

Love. Family. Those for whom their personal life is important will have a great time this wonderful spring month. There is a chance of trips, meeting with your old friends and acquaintances as well as relatives living far away.

However, you are going to have a serious quarrel with one of your family members. You can learn some of your loved ones' secrets and be upset with it. There is another possibility: your loved ones will quarrel with each other, and you will be the only person capable of stopping the conflict.

Relationships between the spouses are calm and stable, just as those between the lovers.

If you are still not married, there is good news for you: you can make an interesting acquaintance, which, most likely, will happen on a trip or when you meet with people who came from far away.

Health. In May, you are energetic and quite healthy, but the stars recommend you to be very careful when traveling and driving a car. The most difficult time is the first tenday period of May.

TAURUS

In May, you are going to overcome another organizational barrier, but after that, the date of the final breakthrough will be close. So keep putting one foot in front of the other.

Job. Career. You won't be very active in the first and second tenday periods. The best thing to do would be preparing the grounds for the decisive breakthrough, which can be expected in the third tenday period.

You can do an important organizational job, tackle the matters you put off for a long time before, analyze the reasons of the failures and learn lessons for the future. You can also clean your office and other work premises.

Relations with colleagues from other cities or countries are uneven, but, in general, the situation has a positive tendency. A trip is possible, when you will be able to combine business with pleasure – relax and renew old partnerships or friendly relations.

In the first half of the month, the employee can definitely go on vacation, while in the second half, he/she can work or look for a new job if the current one doesn't seem good anymore.

Money. This month, you should keep your finance under control. This recommendation is especially important in the first tenday period of May, when there is a chance of big expenses as well as financial losses, thefts and other unpleasant money-related events.

Another option is that a large amount of money will be spent for business, building a house or home renovation.

Love. Family. For many representatives of your sign, the most important events can happen at home, inside the family.

It's possible that you will continue a big renovation, make a decision to move, and in many cases it will be a relocation to another city or country.

At the same time, many of you will allocate some time for themselves as well as spend time with their loved ones; for example, they will have a joint trip, the more so that the traditional May holidays are a very good time for doing that.

Inside the families, relations will be quite harmonious, the friendly couples will be working together to overcome everyday problems and financial difficulties.

For those in love, May is not very good. The stars advise you: Before saying or doing something, smile and count to ten. Perhaps you somewhat exaggerate your problems, which you will understand if you think twice.

Mind that some of your friends are not sincere, not all of them are reliable, so avoid sincere talks and don't lend money. If you do all that, your life will be much easier and calmer.

Health. In May, your energy potential will improve substantially, and this positive tendency will continue in June.

GEMINI

May is not bad for you, but solving the tasks you have set,
related to business and to love, may require a lot of effort.

Job. Career. The first tenday period of May is a very emotional time. You can face your business partners' obvious resistance, which can result in a big conflict. In this regard, the most difficult days are May 4 through 6, when there is a high probability of a serious quarrel.

Don't overestimate yourself and "don't say what you can't unsay". There is a high probability of an unpleasant situation due to harsh words, so speak and act only if you are 100% sure that you are right.

Relations with your friends and high-ranked people are good. Their participation and support will smooth out many of this month's problems and help you in your further undertakings.

Organizational events can be very successful. These include negotiations with banks and other financial institutions, revision of the business, completion of current projects.

The employee can take advantage of the May holidays and relax in the company of his/her loved ones. You will get back in the second half of May and show your best side.

Money. Financial situation is rather contradictory this month. Big expenses are possible in the first half of May; in many cases, they will be related to vacation, trips and parties.

The second half of May is more productive. You will have more money, which will come from various sources.

Love. Family. As to your private life, you are also recommended to control your emotions. In the first tenday period, there is a risk of hurting a loved one with a harsh word. A bit later, you will be sorry for that, so be patient and think twice before speaking. Don't be upset if it seems to you that your loved one is not very sensitive and tactful. Most likely, it is not so.

The singles will have unexpected encounters, meeting with friends and acquaintances as well as pleasant surprises.

Health. In May, your energy potential is not high. Those who have problems with the bronchial and pulmonary system, as well as various forms of allergy, should be especially careful.

CANCER

May is productive and full of events. Quite a number of your projects will be supported by many people. So go ahead!

Job. Career. For the working representatives of your sign, May can turn out to be one of the best months of the year. Initiative, non-standard thinking and the ability to come to terms with others will help the entrepreneurs and the managers to strike deals. The latter ability is your most important feature. Use it, and good luck is guaranteed to you.

The employees can count on a positive attitude of their bosses and support from high-position people.

At the same time, job problems are also possible: the managers and the entrepreneurs should be ready for being audited, while the employees should expect a negative attitude of some of their colleagues.

Most of the problems will happen in the first tenday period of May. If this is the case, don't hesitate to ask your old friends for help. They will provide timely and effective support.

Trips scheduled for May will be rather successful.

Money. This month can bring a significant improvement of your financial situation. It's not about lotteries, winnings and other surprises though. Most likely, successful steps can be taken and wise decisions made, which will soon bring good results.

Love. Family. Your family relations will somewhat improve in May. Taking care of the children, communicating with friends and a joint trip will reconcile the quarreling spouses. All that will distract them from the recent problems and let them look at the situation at a different angle.

It will depend on you whether the fragile peace will last, but there are chances for improvement. It's a good time for making the first step towards your partner, so use one of the few moments left.

Many will renew relationships with their ex lovers and old friends; they will have a chance to revive the old romance and turn the friendly relations into something more significant.

Health. Generally speaking, your energy potential is rather high, but in the first tenday period of May, you may suddenly feel worse. The young and strong people are recommended to avoid traumatic situations, and those suffering chronic diseases – to take preventive measures in order to avoid complications.

LEO

In May, you have a good opportunity to try something new. And the good old foundation won't be an obstacle. On the contrary, it's and obvious and firm plus!

Job. Career. This month is rather good for professional undertakings. The May holidays won't prevent the entrepreneurs and the managers from reviving an old project as well as attracting time-proven colleagues and subordinates.

The employee can have a job offer from an old friend or colleague. Now you know for sure what your goal is to act in strict accordance with the previously developed plan. This makes everything simpler and easier, at least theoretically.

But you can't have the sweet without the sour. This time, "the sour" will be your relations with the colleagues from another city or country, problems with your entourage, or long and boring paperwork.

In each of those three options, the difficulties can be overcome, but you need to assess the situation well and find direct ways for reaching your objective. There is no doubt that those ways exist!

Money. Financially, May is rather contradictory. You will get decent amounts of money on May 14, 15, 22, 23 and at the very end of the month or in early June.

But your expenses will also be high in May. In one case, they will be related to your friends and like-minded people or high-position sponsors, in another, to your children or loved ones.

Love. Family. As to your personal life and romantic relationships, everything is not bad either, especially if love doesn't mean money for you. If something makes you happy and delighted, the amount of money to be paid for it doesn't matter. Do you agree? There is such a conflict between your love and your usual everyday expenses. So think what is more important for you and make a choice. After that, everything will be OK.

The married people having a stable lifestyle can have to spend large amounts of money for their children. But that's important for you, and the money as such doesn't matter.

You must prepare very well for the trips scheduled for the first half of the month. Be especially attentive to all kind of references and documents.

Health. In May, your energy potential is rather high. Even those who fell ill last month will be doing much better in May.

VIRGO

For you, May is a month of motion and change. You can get out of the circle of usual duties and spend time "your way".

Job. Career. This month, the entrepreneurs and the managers will have to change a lot in their business. Perhaps you will have to plunge into the unknown, but you are accustomed to that kind of things: for a long time now, you have been and still are moving your business forward while staying between the devil and the deep sea.

Relations with the business partners are unstable and incomprehensible; it must be the final stage of breaking up with some of them. Do you need to hold what is going away? It's up to you, but a new period is beginning in your life, which means that you have to part with someone or something.

For many, organizational work is on the agenda as well as searching for finance and solving real estate issues.

The trip scheduled for May will be very successful and help you solve numerous issues related to the revival of your business.

The employee can resign and find another place for applying his/her talents. On the other hand, there is a possibility of big changes at the present organization, such as change of the management and system restructuring, which will make the atmosphere in the team quite tense.

Money. There will be more financial problems. They began quite a while ago, and you must have learned to cope with those problems. Now, again, everyone around you will need money, including your children and your partner, so what you get will be lost almost immediately. But bankruptcy is unlikely. Some will be helped by their parents, others will make money due to successful real estate operations, such as sale or rent.

Love. Family. There are problems in your personal life, and this refers both to the spouses and to the lovers. Since the beginning of the month can be very emotional, it is very important to be calm and not to rush. And another piece of advice: Take it easy when spending money. Remember that this is inevitable, while feelings are more important anyway.

Many will finalize renovations or decide to buy a new home at last.

These troublesome events can create problems even for very good and loving couples. If this is the case, remember that all those troubles and tribulations will just make your life better. Besides, the renovation will be over sooner or later, but its results will please you for years to come.

Despite the household problems, the stars strongly advise you to travel to a warm see resort for a week or two. This will reduce the stress and restore peace for the rest of May.

Health. This month, your energy potential is rather high and you will not fall ill.

LIBRA

*May can be called a month of "loneliness" as you will prefer
the narrow circle of your loved ones to team activities and
noisy parties.*

Job. Career. If business is the most important thing in your life, you can dedicate most of May to organizational work as well as to resolving some issues related to land and real estate. When doing this, you can enter into a serious conflict with one of your business partners, which, in the most complicated cases, can result in a big quarrel.

You are accustomed to that, but this time one can say that the balance is tilting in your favor. You will manage to achieve a lot in matters of importance, and this positive process will be finalized towards the end of the year.

Contacts with business partners from other cities or countries will make you feel quite anxious. You will face issues that began long ago, and resolving them will be very difficult. But, as they say, keep putting one foot in front of the other. Do it, and you will reach the goal.

The employee can take a leave and dedicate most of May to solving family problems. He/she will get back to active work not earlier than the third tenday period of May, which is the most successful time for all kinds of professional work.

Money. In terms of finance, May won't be very good for you. It is possible that the expenses will be larger than revenues, so towards the end of the month, the balance will be negative.

Love. Family. In your personal life, the process that began last month will continue. The problematic and divorced spouses will dispute over real estate again, and, after those disputes, which are quite likely in the first tenday period of May, will probably reach at least a relative understanding.

The loving couples will also be engaged in renovation of their homes, and this will bring quite understandable fuss to their lives.

Relations with the relatives are complicated. A serious quarrel is looming among your nearest relatives, and it is highly probable that you will play the role of mediator and arbitrator.

The singles and those disappointed in their affections can expect an interesting encounter and, most likely, it will happen on a trip or when meeting with people who came from far way.

Health. In May, your energy potential is not very high, so the stars strongly recommend you to use the holidays for resting and taking care of yourself.

If a trip is scheduled for the first tenday period of May, it should be prepared carefully. If possible, don't fly on May 5-6. These days are also not good for driving a car.

SCORPIO

The May influences of the stars are rater contradictory for you. But it is now that you will be able to win over those who used to doubt your capabilities.

Job. Career. This month is not bad for professional undertakings. You have a lot of work, and even the May holidays won't be an obstacle for the representatives of your sign.

Relations with business partners from other cities or countries are unstable: something is OK, while something is not. However, in general, these are just working moments, which you should pay more attention to.

There will be a lot of contacts in May; perhaps the old ties will be restored and new acquaintances appear.

You are guaranteed to have everyone's attention to your work, and this is the major component of success.

The entrepreneurs and the managers will strike profitable deals, while the employees can count on more assignments and salary increases.

Money. In terms of finance, this month is not bad at all. The money will be coming on a regular basis and its amount will be growing significantly. The estimated dates for getting the most substantial amounts are May 2, 3, 11-13, 20, 21.

However, in early May, you will have to make unexpected expenses. In this respect, the difficult days are May 5-8, when serious expenses, thefts and financial losses are quite probable. Those whose work is somehow related to finance - accountants, bankers or brokers, should be especially cautious. To minimize the losses, they must take into account all possible risks.

The married people will mostly spend money for their children.

Love. Family. You will be in high spirits and optimistic throughout May, that's why quite a lot of people will seek your advice. In May, especially in its second half, you will make new acquaintances, which is an excellent chance to make new friends and, perhaps, change your life.

You will renew relations with your old friends and ex-partners living in other cities or countries. In a word, the choice is guaranteed, which is good for the singles, but can bring many problems to those who have a partner.

Relations with your relatives will be much more active; it is possible that you will meet with the relatives living in another city or country.

Those married will have problems with their children, and big expenses are quite probable.

Health. Towards the end of the month, numerous contacts and a lot of fuss can make you exhausted. So it would be a good idea to take a short vacation and go to a warm place. If you can't do it, don't forget to make breaks and spend the weekends out of town.

SAGITTARIUS

Nothing can make you stop working, neither the May holidays nor the numerous parties. Your main advantages - stress resistance and restlessness - will let you win all the battles!

Job. Career. This month, you will be overwhelmed with your new job and new ideas. They are very promising and can bring a good income quickly.

At the same time, the stars say that the basis of the current undertakings will be exactly what you were recently engaged in, so some conservatism will do you good. What can be more stable and reliable than a new business on the old basis? Be courageous, success is guaranteed.

However, you must be strong and patient in May, because you will have to do a lot all by yourself, not trusting your entourage.

The whole picture can be somewhat spoiled by conflicts with some of your business partners. This situation, which began long ago, will get aggravated in the first tenday period of May.

Money. In terms of finance, this month is not bad at all. The money will be received regularly and its amount will increase significantly.

The estimated dates for getting the most substantial amounts are May 4, 5, 14, 15, 21-23.

There will be few expenses, they will be mostly related to your personal life, the holidays, the needs of your children or your partner.

Love. Family. This month is not very good for your personal life; both lovers and spouses will have conflicts.

You are energetic, ambitious, but some people won't like it, so cool off. These recommendations are relevant throughout the month, especially in the first tenday period, when a careless word can result in a serious conflict. In many cases, the reason will be real estate, and this is mainly a problem of the spouses.

The children will please you most of the time, but you will have to allocate a large amount of the family budget for their needs.

Health. In May, you will have a lot of responsibilities, so towards the end of May you will probably not feel very confident and cheerful. Since you can hardly forget about your job completely, try to rest more and take care of yourself.

CAPRICORN

You are always too busy to waste time dreaming. But this month, you will have a few days and maybe even a week to feel a romantic daydreamer. And you will find this period very pleasant!

Job. Career. The first week of May isn't very good for business, and many will spend it far away from home.

At the same time, the managers and the self-employed are recommended to be more attentive to what their junior partners and subordinates are doing, and control them. Some of them can be too active and behave like a bull in a china shop.

You should also be ready for an unexpected audit.

Relations with the colleagues from other cities and countries will become much more stable exclusively due to your efforts. You should keep this sphere of your activities under your personal control as there is no one who could help you in doing that.

May is very good for people of creative professions. They can have excellent ideas, which will be implemented very quickly.

In the first half of the month, the employees will take care of their careers and, perhaps, will travel to a warm sea resort. But in general, the above recommendations are important for them, too.

Money. In terms of finance, May is not very good. There will be a lot of expenses, while the income will be somewhat lower. The exclusions are the constructors and those whose business has something to do with real estate. In this area, a certain revival is expected, which will affect the finance immediately: you will have much more money.

Love. Family. May is very good for personal life. Talking about your own feelings is a nightmare for you. In this sphere, you are not sincere and natural, but this is the only way to live "your way". Perhaps you will understand this and get rid of the frame you once put yourself in, which your partner will like very much.

May is a good time for the singles and those disappointed in their former affections. You will have new acquaintances and find excellent possibilities to reorganize your personal life.

Those married will keep improving their homes. There is a chance of a big renovation, buying new furniture and other things that make everyday life beautiful.

Relations with your children will be much better; a new, positive turn in their lives is possible.

Your complicated relations with the relatives will be somewhat more stable. Most likely, it will be you who will make the first step in their direction, which will be quite adequate this time.

Health. In general, your energy potential is high this month and you will be healthy. But be careful on May 5 through 10 when driving, and try to avoid dangerous situations.

AQUARIUS

This month, your comfort zone is your home and country house as well as maybe your "dream trip". But it would be better to do all that when you are surrounded by your loved ones.

Job. Career. The best thing the professionally active representatives of your sign can do this month is to renew the ties with their friends as well as with people of high social positions.

Many will travel in order to meet with their friends living in other cities or countries.

The entrepreneurs and the managers will do some reorganization, such as renovation in the office and other premises. Some will have ideas of expanding the business and making related acquisitions.

Many will consider starting their own business, and this idea will be implemented in the near future.

The employee will take a few days off and, in the first half of the month, take care of his/her private life.

Money. In terms of finance, this month won't be stable. Your children and loved ones will need money; besides, there will be substantial expenses aimed at solving organizational as well as household problems.

The complicated issues related to your friends or high-ranked people will be settled gradually, but some issues will remain unresolved, and you will have to tackle them later on.

Love. Family. In May, many representatives of your sign will be busy solving their personal problems.

Those married will put things in order in their country house, do renovation or maybe begin looking for a new home.

The children will require a lot of attention as the adults will have business or personal problems. The little ones may behave arrogantly, be uncontrollable, or suddenly fall ill.

For those in love, this month won't be easy. In early May, serious disagreements and quarrels are possible. The stars advise you to keep your emotions under control and not pay attention to small things.

But if you have a dispute concerning your differing value systems or, God forbid, money, think twice if your partner is really the person you need.

Health. In May, you will be quite healthy, but there may be a weight gain tendency, so don't forget to exercise and fast.

pISCes

May has gifts in store for you: moving, changing and all kinds of improvements. Don't restrain your fantasy and spend time your way.

Job. Career. In the first half of May, the best idea would be taking a short leave and traveling to a warm place.

And if your business is more important for you, nothing will prevent you from combining it with pleasure: while having a rest, you can talk business with your friends.

You will renew the old ties; there is a chance of meeting with your friend and high-position people living in other cities and countries.

Besides, in the second half of May, you will have new acquaintances, which will influence very well your long-range and close plans and undertakings. There is a chance that you will have a job offer from somewhere far from your home, and, later on, you will think of relocation. Another option is frequent business trips.

The employee will have a golden opportunity to strengthen his/her position at the recently received place. If this didn't happen, you can try to find a new job. In any variant, the influence of the stars on your career is positive.

You are proactive, have non-standard thinking and can meet your colleagues half way. Even if you don't get promoted, the boss will be definitely impressed with your qualities.

Money. Your financial situation will also improve. You will start getting money on a regular basis, the estimated dates of getting the biggest amounts being May 2, 3, 11–13, 20, 21, 29, 30.

Love. Family. Pleasant surprises are also possible in your personal life. The stars recommend those searching for a good partner not to miss a single party and be well dressed as the probability of new acquaintances is rather high this month. In some cases, this will happen on a trip or among people who came from far away.

Throughout the month, you will be surrounded by all kinds of people, such as your old friends as well as those who have power and money. Just don't get confused and choose what you really need.

Changes at home are also possible, such as renovation, buying things that make your everyday life more beautiful, and other events that will keep you busy. This can confuse the spouses and they will quarrel more than they usually do.

Relations with the relatives will be more active, there is a chance of traveling to another city or country to meet with some of them.

Health. This month, you are healthy, cheerful, energetic and very attractive, which will be noticed by everyone you will come across.

JUNE

ARIES

Don't turn off your path! Don't be afraid of being criticized, and pay no attention to the obstacles. The stars show that you are moving in the right direction. "To infinity and beyond!" – this is your motto!

Job. Career. You are in for a difficult time, when each step will be hard to make. The entrepreneurs and managers will face an unpredictable position of their partners from other cities and countries and make the same mistake twice.

In the most complicated situations, the collaboration may stop temporarily, which is hard to predict in a general forecast. But the stars show that you will manage to collaborate with some of your business partners, though not with others.

It is possible that your colleagues won't find common grounds either and have a big quarrel. If this is the case, think twice before starting to be a moderator or an arbitrator as there is a risk of spoiling relations with both parties. Besides, it is possible that you don't have full information, so, again, think twice before saying or doing something.

The same is recommended to the employee, who can face a problem at work. The reason can be an intricate intrigue dating back to the past.

In case of legal problems, it's highly probable that they will get aggravated this month.

Money. In terms of finance, June will probably not be good, which is quite natural taking into account the state of your business. But you made some money last month of course, and this will help you now.

Love. Family. Those for whom their personal life is important will also face difficulties. Many families will have conflicts with their relatives, and the problems can be extremely emotional from both sides. The quarrel among you and your relatives has been looming since long ago, but this time, it's about real estate or another kind of large property. Each party will be defending their own position, and a consensus is unlikely this month.

In extreme situations, the case can go to court. This, as well as other things, will make the atmosphere in the family rather disturbing. Those "other things" can include your personal problems related to disputed property, which you will have to solve somehow.

As to the lovers, it's hard to say something definite about them, but, with this position of the stars, they will hardly have a calm June.

Trips, including private and business trips, scheduled for this month can be unsuccessful, so it would be better to cancel them unless there is an emergency.

Health. In June, you are healthy and energetic, though extremely nervous and restless. If you can't lower the stress, take at least a good sleep, and don't forget about exercising and outdoor walking.

The drivers are recommended to be especially cautious throughout the month.

TAURUS

*The main motto of June is "Money likes being counted".
If you act accordingly, you will be able to improve your
situation and lower the probability of losses.*

Job. Career. Situations you are going to face in June are similar to those you have faced before.

Most likely, certain financial obligations will be involved. Once more, your opponents will be your friends or some high-position people you had the imprudence to deal with.

Another option is investing big money in complex operations related to expanding your business as well as to real estate. In this case, your hope for someone's help may not come true and you will have to use your own money only.

Many problems that arise this month can have a legal continuation, so make sure that you have all necessary documents as well as good lawyers.

Relations with your colleagues from other cities and countries are also far from being ideal. All kinds of conflicts are possible in mid June. It is not excluded that you will have to resort to the help of one of your business partners to solve those problems.

Money. Money outflow can be really huge this month. Except business investments and debt obligations, thefts and big financial losses are possible. This should be taken into account by all representatives of your sign whose job has something to do with money, such as accountants, brokers, bankers, and dealers. Exclude any risk in June. It should be absolutely out of the question as its results will be definitely very bad.

Those who have nothing to do with business will have to spend money for solving various family problems, and the expenses will be much higher than expected.

Love. Family. Many representatives of your sign will have to forget about love and romantics due to the numerous professional and financial problems. But those whose life is full of emotions are recommended to be especially cautious in June and "walk on tiptoes."

Your loved one can be stubborn and annoyed, so you are recommended not to pester him/her with requests, to say nothing of accusations. You won't be understood. But if you begin to lose patience, follow the Biblical commandment of humbleness. If you are a non-believer, meditations and yoga will help you.

Relations with your relatives will not be ideal either, a sudden quarrel is possible in mid June. However, it will be about old accusations and grievances.

Health. Those who will have no professional and personal troubles, may have health problems. Take more care of your body, especially if you had problems in the past.

In mid June, be careful on the trips and when driving a car as there is a high probability of injures and accidents in this period.

GEMINI

There are periods when usual actions stop bringing usual results. Never say die! And don't try to break the wall, which may turn out to be unbreakable. Look for non-standard roundabout ways!

Job. Career. In terms of business, this is rather a contradictory period. The problem has been looming for a long time, and you should now analyze the situation and set things straight.

Once more it's about your relations with some of your business partners who are trying to play according to their own rules. You may be displeased with the attitude of your colleagues to your joint business as well as the distribution of money.

This month, a compromise is out of the question, the conflicts can be very tough. So think twice before starting a battle – is fighting really necessary? But if it is, don't be afraid of defending your position as strength and perseverance are now more important than gentleness and diplomacy.

The employee can face the same situation; he/she is in for serious battles with the competitors as well as for conflicts with the boss.

Money. In June, making money will require fighting, but the result will be good! The stars show that you will manage to get if not all the money your business partners owe you then at least most of it.

Those who will have no professional troubles, will have to face misunderstanding with the loved one.

Love. Family. If your personal life is your priority, your will have some difficulties this month. A relationship which used to be important for you will become a burden. The general forecast can't tell you the reason, but the separation process is definitely underway.

One option is that you will like another person, in which case the previous relationship will be over. Another option is that it will be your partner who will find someone else. But in either case, financial issues will also be involved, which will make the situation still more complicated.

It is definitely related to those who had problems in the past, while the new unions will not face such difficulties.

Health. This month, your energy potential isn't high. Besides, there is a chance of accidents, injuries, etc. Be especially prudent in mid June, which is the most problematic period.

CANCER

This month is very difficult for you. You need to be careful and "walk on tiptoes." You can face all kinds of problems, so defend!

Job. Career. You can face business problems that have been looming since long ago.

The entrepreneurs and managers are recommended to get ready in advance for the highly probable audits. Besides, there will be a problem with one the business partners.

The sharpest conflicts are likely to happen in mid June; the most complicated cases will be brought to court. If this happens to you, don't let things take their course. Hire experienced lawyers instead, because the situation is really complicated.

The employee can get into an intricate intrigue and lose his/her positions at work.

All representatives of this sign should take into account that some secrets can be made public this month, which will influence negatively your reputation and the attitude of your entourage to you. So be prudent and cover your bases!

Money. The financial situation is not quite clear. Your professional problems won't affect your finance, at least for the time being.

You can expect getting some money on June 8, 9, 16, 17, 25–27. There will be numerous expenses, but all of them are predictable and reasonable.

Love. Family. Various situations are possible in your personal life. The spouses who have problems will again start talking about separation. The influence of the relatives will partly though not fully improve the situation.

Something that you want to keep secret can be revealed this month, so be prudent and don't share your secrets with those you don't trust.

The same recommendations are relevant for the lovers.

Health. Those who will have no professional and personal troubles, may have health problems. This month, your chronic diseases can remind you of themselves. You should get ready for that in advance.

All kinds of unpleasant events are possible this month, so don't walk alone along dark streets, be careful on the trips and when driving a car. In this regard, mid June is the most dangerous time.

LEO

June will put very sensitive questions before you about your relations with many people. Remember that not all processes can be in your favor.

Job. Career. This month, you can depend on your entourage. In particular, the entrepreneurs and the managers will have conflicts with their friends or high position people about finance and general development of the business.

There is a probability of audits that will reveal some flaws, in particular in finance. So get ready for the future events and remember that very serious problems are possible.

The managers are recommended to be more attentive to the subordinates as some of the latter are not quite loyal.

The employee is likely to have conflicts with some of his/her hostile colleagues, as well as intrigues inside the team.

All representatives of your sign should bear in mind that some unpleasant secrets can be revealed in June and July, which will have an obviously negative effect on your reputation. So cover your bases!

Money. Financially, June won't be very stable, all kinds of expenses are possible. Some will spend a lot of money to solve their family problems, others will have to pay off their debts to their friends or resolve issues with high-position persons.

Love. Family. In your personal life, you can also find yourself in a difficult situation. The lovers will discover suddenly that their views can differ very much. In the best-case scenario, those will be emotional disputes, jealousy, or unexpected information concerning each other's past.

In the worst-case one, financial claims are possible, resulting in a serious quarrel.

You will want greatly to have the last say, and "that say" will be very sharp.

The married people are likely to have problems with their children, which can result in big expenses that will weaken the family budget seriously.

Health. In June, many will face rater unexpected problems. In the middle of the month, the elderly and weakened people can experience exacerbations of chronic illnesses. Those who suffer diseases of the musculoskeletal system and diseases of the gastrointestinal tract should be especially prudent.

Mid June is a very traumatic period, so be careful and avoid risky situations.

VIRGO

In June, you will act as a leader, and this will help you solve many business and personal problems.

Job. Career. In June, many representatives of your sign risk to find themselves in a controversial situation related to their friends or high-position people. The problem can be the different approaches to the joint business, money or other material values. The sharpest conflicts will happen in the middle of the month, but there will be nothing new about them as you have already faced that more than once.

At the same time, you will have good relations with your colleagues from other cities or countries; interesting offers and vast assistance are probable.

Trips scheduled for early June will be successful.

The employee will have additional assignments, which will cause envy of the competing colleagues, but improve relations with the boss.

All representatives of your sign should remember that this month, many controversial issues will be resolved in your favor, so go ahead boldly!

Money. Your financial situation will become somewhat better, but it won't be quite stable. You have numerous expenses – a tradition that shaped several years ago. Those expenses include old debts, the children's requirements, and business problems.

This time, all kinds of needs will take most of the money you have received.

Love. Family. In June, many representatives of your sign will be overwhelmed with work at home and at work. There are problems with the renovation of the new home, which you want to solve until fall. But this month, you will be distracted by the children, the work, and the partner, so the issues of the new home will be apparently put off till better times.

The couples who have problematic relationships are likely to have serious conflicts and quarrels in the middle of the month. In another variant, the loved one can fall ill or experience bad times, which will make the atmosphere in the family rather tense.

The children will have problems, too, and your help will be required, both moral and material.

June will also be rather complicated for the lovers. The astrologer thinks that a separation process has long been going on in your life. What is happening is a long-time, but perhaps necessary step, and when everything is left behind, you will immediately feel better. The June events can show the situation "in all its glory", and the stars advise you not to hold what wants to go away.

Health. In June, your energy potential is rather high, which will let you face adequately all the situations taking place during this complicated month.

LIBRA

For a long time you can't get out of a vicious circle of the same problems. One of the reasons can be that you observe the rules of the game, while your opponents don't even know that the game has rules.

Job. Career. The agenda will also include problems with your business partners from other cities and countries as well as controversial issues related to land and other real estate property. Your aggressive competitors can cross dangerous borders, especially in mid June. In this period, the conflicts will be off the chain. But you can't retreat because, as they say, "if you give them a finger, they'll bite your whole hand off." So defend and retaliate, from time to time.

Besides, the entrepreneurs and the managers are recommended to be very attentive with their subordinates: at best, they are just passive; at worst, they tell you lies or, for some reasons, play their own game.

The employee can have problems with his/her colleagues, intrigues inside the team, rumors and gossip. Stay away from that and do your job in the best way possible, because this month, there is a high probability of conflicts with your boss.

Another option: the organization is changing, which will lead to unrest in the team, rumors and unhealthy competition of team members.

Money. Despite some business issues, there will be no financial problems, at least for the time being. The largest amounts will be received on June 1, 6, 7, 13, 14.

Love. Family. This will be a problematic period for the families. Conflicts with relatives will begin or continue in many families, and practically all family members will be involved.

The subject of the dispute may be a house/apartment or anther property, but thanks to your efforts, the situation will be changing in your favor.

The peaks of the conflict will occur in mid June, when the masks will be dropped and the situation will show itself "in all its glory." If you have to go to court, don't save on a lawyer.

Health. This month, your energy potential is high enough and you will cope with all the personal and business issues.

SCORPIO

In June, the planets can seriously limit your capabilities. So don't rush to make a decision and remember that slow and steady wins the race.

Job. Career. This month, your professional interests may contradict those of other people. The discrepancies can relate to finance, and in the most difficult cases, you may go to court.

The managers and the entrepreneurs are recommended to get ready for audits, which are highly probable this month.

Those who have ties with their colleagues living in other cities and countries, will also face some difficulties. For various reasons, the collaboration can become more complicated or just stop.

In this difficult period, you will have "a little help from your friends" or from some of the loyal business partners.

The employee is recommended to go on vacation and do his/her personal things; if this is impossible, the stars recommend you to stay away from any intrigues, and listen instead of speaking.

Money. Financial problems are possible in June. There will be a lot of expenses, while the income will somewhat go down. But your financial difficulties won't result in bankruptcy – in a couple of months, you will have back what you lost.

Love. Family. More often than not, your decisions in love affairs are caused by the fact that you are trying to understand whether you can connect your life with this or that person and be happy with him/her. Now this decision is particularly difficult to make due to numerous financial and everyday factors.

Is it possible to measure love by money? It's up to you to decide, but you seem to be able to afford that. The only thing needed is your wish.

Many families will face problems with the relatives. In mid June, a serious quarrel will break out among the nearest relatives, which may affect all your family members.

The children will not only be the reason for the conflict, but also require serious financial expenses. Try to understand the problems of your older children and take care of the younger ones' health. It is very important in June!

Your spouse or a faithful loved one will support you throughout this difficult month, always on time.

Health. Those who won't face professional and personal troubles may have health problems.

June is not just difficult, but also traumatic. The worst period will be from June 10 through June 20, when the probability of extreme situations is rather high. Be especially careful when traveling and driving!

SAGITTARIUS

In June, you will understand that there are people in your entourage who disagree with you completely, and there are also those whose attitude to you is quite hostile. Well, nothing can be done about it. That's life.

Job. Career. A difficult period begins in your business matters. You are constantly facing resistance, which is absolutely groundless in some cases. Conflicts with your business partners are possible, the main reason being, as it usually happens, money or big property, such as real estate. The biggest conflicts can be expected in mid June, and your business partners will hardly want to meet you halfway. On the other hand, there is no sense for you in making concessions either, so the situation can come to a standstill.

The stars recommend you to persevere to the end and finally accept what is almost unacceptable. In any case, Jupiter is on your side, which means that your positions are stronger.

Your opponents are stubborn, but they will have to make concessions or stop collaborating with you. Before making a decision, assess the situation. Perhaps you can cope with everything on your own and need no partners like that.

The more so that you have a job, maybe your own business, and good assistants.

Money. The financial situation is rather contradictory. On the one hand, you have enough money, but on the other, there are many expenses. In one case, they are related to your business, in another, to your personal life. It depends, as they say.

Love. Family. In the personal life, it is very important to be realistic about your capabilities.

The new opportunities given to you by Jupiter can make you feel dizzy, which will have a negative effect on the existing ties. Your partner or another loved one can make claims to you, and they will be fair in many cases.

If it is about the people who recently appeared in your entourage, think twice if you can rely on them and whether it is a good idea to break a long-standing, stable tie because of them. It's up to you, of course, but try to be reasonable and use common sense.

If you break up with your partner, please mind that you will have to face property division.

Health. In June, your energy potential is low, but if you remember about the importance of having a rest and sleep well, you will avoid serious illnesses.

CAPRICORN

Nothing stays hidden for long, and you will make sure of that in June. You are the strongest sign of the Zodiac, so keep the defense!

Job. Career. If the basis of your life is your job, business, professional relations, you should get ready for two problems, quite probable during this troubled month.

One is the audits, which can reveal all the shortcomings of your activity, both imaginary and real.

The other one is related to the attitude of some of your partners, who are perhaps not happy with the direction of the business and your unyielding position.

The middle of the month will be the toughest time, but, most likely, this will not be the end of your troubles and tribulations, which may resume later on.

Those who have connections abroad can face an uncertain position of their foreign colleagues. For several reasons, the collaboration may be interrupted or seriously complicated.

Besides, the managers and the entrepreneurs are recommended to pay attention to their subordinates: quite a lot may depend on this in this difficult month.

Changes are underway at the organization where the employee works, that's why the atmosphere can be disturbing and tense. There is a high probability of intrigues, fake information, rumors and gossip. Do you best not to get lost in this whirlpool and remember that "silence is golden."

Money. Your financial situation looks uncertain, which is not surprising in this scenario. But bankruptcy is unlikely, which is good news.

Love. Family. Those for whom personal life is a priority will also face difficulties in June. The problematic couples can start warfare once again; the most ruinous battles will happen in the middle of the month.

Jealousy, resentment, problems of the past can become the topic of June, and if you have some secrets, be ready that they will be revealed.

Living will be easier for the lovers – the sky promises "green light" to them.

Relations with your relatives are quite complicated, but you can settle everything, or, rather, clarify the situation provoked by some of your relatives and help them cope with various problems.

Health. Those who won't face professional and personal troubles may have health problems. In June, there is a probability of exacerbation of chronic diseases and unexpected appearance of new ones. In the middle of the month, be more careful when traveling and driving.

AQUARIUS

In June, you will face another challenge. But you will cope with it: you have been staying between the devil and the deep see for a long time now and, despite that, you keep moving your business forward.

Job. Career. This month, an unpleasant situation is likely, which you need to get ready for in advance. Auditors can be interested in your work, and it will be very serious.

Besides, finance-related conflicts with your friends and some high-position people are likely, each party having their own opinion. In this difficult period, you will be supported by your family and your loved ones, including your spouse, parents and senior family members.

In general, your positions will be quite solid, and you will manage to overcome the troubles one way or another, if not in June, then a bit later.

Money. In June, the financial situation is rather complicated, money will be spent for quite different reasons. Some of you will be ruined by professional matters, others will have expenses related to their children and loved ones.

Love. Family. Your personal life will probably not be smooth. Relations with the children will get worse, mutual accusations and grievances are possible. In another version, your adult children can have problems in personal life or business, while the younger children will require more attention and care. In any event, a substantial portion of the family budget will be spent for the children's needs.

June will also be difficult for the lovers: you will have to understand whether this is a serious relationship or just a one-day craze.

It's time to answer this question now that the first problems are arising. Perhaps you will come to the conclusion that the perspectives are not rosy.

Health. In June, your energy potential is rather high, but unexpected accidents and injuries are possible. In this regard, the most difficult time is mid June, when the probability of unpleasant events is rather high.

In the same period, the weak and the elderly can experience aggravation of old chronic diseases.

pisces

You need to spend June in a quiet and isolated place, such as a monastery or a closed sanatorium. If you don't do this, the first summer month will bring you various problems.

Job. Career. June is not very good for working. Many representatives of your sign should take a two-week vacation and focus on personal and family-related matters. But this mainly refers to the employees; as to the entrepreneurs and the managers, the stars don't recommend them to let things take their course. June is not bad for various organizational matters as well as for solving problems that were put off till "better times".

The first half of the month is a good time for strengthening the ties with your old friends and colleagues living in other cities and countries. A successful trip is possible this month.

The stars recommend the employees who keep working to be more modest, not put forward any unnecessary initiatives and by all means abstain from criticizing the boss. You won't be understood in any case.

Money. In terms of finance, June is most likely quite neutral. You can't expect a big income, but all your expenses will be predictable and reasonable.

Love. Family. In your personal life, various events are possible, most of which have happened before.

In particular, the warring couples can quarrel again when dividing property, first of all real estate.

Those in love can face problems and unexpected obstacles. Perhaps you will find out that your relationship doesn't have rosy perspectives. Anyway, a quarrel, quite probable in mid June, can put an end to the illusions, which the representatives of your sign are prone to.

Problems with the children are quite probable for the parents in this difficult period.

Relations with the relatives are quite harmonious, and perhaps the loved ones will support you when you have a difficult time.

And something else: Your solid, philosophical and peacemaking position can help you find a way out of many problems posed by this very hard month. Listen to your inner voice and don't give in to provocations.

Health. In June, your energy potential is not high. Many will have a weight gain tendency, so don't forget about exercising in the morning, and walk a lot.

JULY

ARIES

There are difficult periods, when it is quite necessary to stop, look around and cover your bases. This is what July is about.

Job. Career. In professional matters, a dead season has begun. Mercury is moving backwards, which means that the people you need will disappear from the horizon and you will require a short rest. It may seem to you that the weight you are carrying is too heavy and you can't cope with it. This is a temporary situation though: you are strong enough and will resume fighting in 4-6 weeks.

But now, in a "quiet mode", you can do organizational work and tackle the tasks you used to put off for various reasons.

The employee can consider looking for a new job; the corresponding opportunities will appear towards the fall. Meanwhile, you can think everything over and ask your soul what exactly it wants.

Money. In July, the financial situation can't be called stable. Expenses, mostly related to the needs of your family and children, will be never-ending.

Love. Family. For most of the representatives of your sign, July is a month of serious changes in the everyday life, that is construction or renovation, in which many of your family members will be involved. In some cases, this will happen far from your home and cost you a pretty penny.

The children bring you not only joy, but also big expenses. Perhaps you will have to limit them in some aspects, which seems quite right to the astrologer.

If you dream of a short vacation or an interesting trip, your dream may come true in late July: you can travel somewhere you have already been to more than once. Many will go to see their relatives and parents, meet with their old friends and people they haven't seen for a long time.

Difficult relations with the relatives will be settled gradually or just become less tense, which is also not bad.

Health. In July, your energy potential is not high, and this is a good time for taking care of yourself. Walk, read your favorite books, watch good movies, and have a good sleep of course! In a word, spend time the way you always wanted to!

TAURUS

This month, you will mostly succeed in finalizing what you began earlier and correcting your mistakes. So good luck!

Job. Career. You are still having a rough time in your business. Those who are facing legal problems will be searching for the necessary information and arguments, and backing them up with facts.

Don't be sad if all the events you have planned will be moving much slower than expected. Most likely, you will have to analyze the situation, which requires time.

Relations with the colleagues from other cities or countries are still complicated. You will need 6-8 weeks to clarify and normalize them, so don't rush and study all the details of what is going on. This is the best thing you can do now!

Also, be very attentive to the documents as they can play an important role in all the matters of this complicated month.

All representatives of your sign, no matter what kind of job they are doing, should take into account that any rush will be bad now. July is the time of realizing and correcting your mistakes. As to other people's mistakes, leave them alone since you can do nothing about them.

Money. You are still having financial problems, but, after reviewing your expenses, you will definitely find out sources of big savings, which will help you feel more confident. Besides, a small amount of money may hit your account in early July, so you will be able to survive this month.

Love. Family. You are facing the same problems in your personal life. Relations with the relatives are far from ideal; you are recommended to avoid conflicts, to say nothing of provoking them. Clarifying relations is likely, and you must approach it with a cold head. Otherwise, all family members will be involved in the conflict, which will make the situation still worse.

Another situation is also possible: Some of your nearest relatives will have conflicts and you will have to be the arbitrator.

Besides, you will have problems inside your family. In particular, you will need to finalize the renovation, clear the summer house, or help your elderly parents.

The lovers who quarrelled in June will perhaps think of reconciliation and make initial steps in this direction. One thing is clear - there is still something left between you, and you will want to discuss it.

Health. In July, your energy potential will be somewhat better, but the stars still recommend you to be careful when driving.

The difficult period is July 8 through 16.

GEMINI

In July, you can find yourself in a difficult situation. Perhaps you will have to make a step back in order to move forward. Cheer up! The problems will end in early August.

Job. Career. The last month problems will continue. It's still about the unsettled financial matters, which you will have to deals with throughout July. Unexpected bad news is quite possible in early July, which will make you look at the problem from a different angle and analyze it more carefully.

At the same time, you will see that the situation is changing for the better, slowly but steadily. So analyze it, take aim, and act without rush.

Relations with your colleagues living in other cities and countries will become somewhat more complicated. Perhaps you will need to get back to analyzing some controversial financial issues and update the existing agreements.

The employee will have better relations with his/her boss, which will have positive financial consequences. At the same time, the stars still recommend you to be cautious with your colleagues, not tell your secrets and avoid intrigue.

Money. You financial situation will improve as the result of the huge job you did before.

The last weeks must have passed in a fierce battle for something that, in your opinion, belongs to you and nobody else, and every successful attack required a lot of your effort. But every step forward makes your enemy retreat and brings you closer to victory.

If you keep acting like that, you will gradually achieve your goal.

Love. Family. If personal life is your priority, you will have to tackle complicated financial problems.

This refers to those who have long been living "in a war mode" and are ready for divorce and property division. This month, you can come to terms with your partner and get from him/her what, as you think, belongs to you. It won't be easy, but nothing is impossible, and the balance leans toward you anyway.

Relations with the relatives will be somewhat more complicated; unexpected problems are probable in early July. Pay close attention to them as they may appear again later on. Something else is possible, too: One of your relatives will be sick or experience other problems; he/she will need support, both financial and moral.

The new relationship is successful, marriage is probable.

Health. In July, your energy potential is not high. People suffering chronic gastrointestinal tract diseases should be especially cautious.

In early July, be very careful on trips and when driving.

CANCER

Your position will become stronger in early July, and you will be able to introduce your own rules of the game. Don't hurry! Time is working for you.

Job. Career. This month, the planets obviously support you. You feel strong and confident, you are ready for the challenges life has in store for you. These qualities will help you solve the problems with the business partners who have long been trying to appropriate the results of your work. In all probability, after all the conflicts and useless fighting, the time has come to start negotiations. Many in your entourage are going to support you.

In the event of legal problems, there will be a chance of a peaceful solution. So take that chance! If you need mediators, you will definitely find them.

Relations with the colleagues from other cities or countries will gradually normalize. There is a possibility of negotiations, which will result in a way out of the complicated situations of the previous month.

Money. Your financial situation will also be better, a decent amount will hit your account in the period from July 21 through July 26. In early July, unexpected expenses are possible, while on July 1-6, you may lose some money.

Love. Family. There will be improvements in your personal life. Your partner's demands are not likely to decrease, but your patience seems to be coming to an end. Your relatives will influence the situation in a positive way, but fail to resolve all the issues.

A lot of problems have accumulated. They can break through like an avalanche, and it doesn't matter what the last straw will be. The eruption of the volcano would have happened sooner or later anyway, but this can be the decisive moment.

This refers not only to the couples having a long experience of common problems, but also to those who are used to talking about divorce.

Health. In July, your energy potential will improve, and even those who fell ill last month will be getting better very quickly.

LEO

In July, you will have a good chance to regroup your forces and get ready for an offense, which is quite probable next month.

Job. Career. July is not very good for doing business. The problems that appeared last month will persist, and each step will require a lot of effort.

You are in an incredible situation: there is not a single way forward. The stars recommend you not to try and destroy the walls with your forehead, the more so that those walls may turn out to be made of armed concrete, but, rather, take your time and analyze the situation. This month, you should act carefully, prudently and quietly, otherwise you can infuriate those people whose positions are much stronger.

The employees are recommended not to make claims to the boss, although they will be clearly prone to do that in early July. The answer to the questions and appeals can be very sharp and negative.

Those who face audits and legal problems should get ready for the logical continuation of those problems. You will have to search for and finalize the documents required by the law, as well as ask your friends to help you.

All representatives of your sign, no matter what they do for a living, should mind that the usual ways can be blocked now, but there are some almost invisible paths, which will bring you to success.

Money. Your financial situation is not stable, which is only natural with this structure of your professional activity. Analyze your expenses and find savings options, which you definitely have. Please mind that you can only expect a serious amount of money in fall.

Love. Family. Those whose priority is personal life, will also face some difficulties this month. Some of your loved ones can be sick or have a hard time, so your comprehensive support will be required. Your loved ones who are in trouble will be extremely grateful to you, if not now, then later on.

The lovers can face a complex intrigue, so they need to think twice before telling someone their secret. Remember that silence is golden and act accordingly.

These recommendations are also relevant for many representatives of your sign despite their marital status and occupation.

Health. Those who have no business difficulties may have health problems. This month, you are in the "bad luck zone" in many aspects, so take care and remember that everything will end sooner or later, while the health and nerves spent to solve various problems can't be restored.

If you don't feel well, see the doctors you trust, and don't spare time for rest.

VIRGO

*This month, you will do your best to defend your positions –
and you will succeed!*

Job. Career. In July, normalization of the difficult situation with your business partners will begin. Perhaps some of your friends or high-position sponsors will help you and act as mediators between you and your opponents. This will be an effective step that will help you find a compromise.

Don't be upset if something goes on slower this month than you want. Mercury, your governor, is moving backwards, so don't rush things. Just take your time to review your business matters and analyze your problems.

In the first tenday period, be ready for an unpleasant surprise from one of your former business partners living somewhere far away. In another variant, fulfilment of mutual obligations can be hampered by force majeure.

The employee who has lost his/her professional positions can ask his/her friends for help: in one case, he/she will get a new job, in another – retain the current job.

Money. This month, your financial positions are not stable. You will be constantly spending money; in one case, the expenses will be related to your job, in another – to your personal life, your family and your children's needs.

Love. Family. In your personal life, the processes that began earlier will persist.

The lovers are still displeased with each other, and the showdown seems to be too time-consuming. In any case, you should take into account that your partner is not going to change, so even if you do your best to restore the relationship, there is a chance of similar problems in the future.

If you are ready for that, accept the conditions. If not, it would be better to set the record straight. In the future, you will have a lot of opportunities to change your life.

The parents will have to keep solving their children's problems, but there is no other way out: who if not you?

The friendly spouses are busy improving their and their children's homes. The renovation may be finished in August.

Health. This month, your energy potential is high enough and you won't be sick.

LIBRA

This month, you will take the last month's difficult situation under your full control. The battle is not over yet, although the advantage is on your side now.

Job. Career. All professionally active representatives of your sign will be working hard during the coming weeks as well as fighting a lot. Although the problems of the last months are still vital and each step forward requires much effort, you have a chance to solve the problems.

In particular, the issues you have with your business partners living in other cities and countries are losing their acuteness; constructive negotiations will be possible towards the end of July. Perhaps some of your friends or some high-position people will help you about that.

Besides, you will have better relations with your assistants and subordinates. It seems that you are putting things in order in your ranks.

But there will still be controversial situations with your business partners related to the mutual property, most likely land or real estate. The problem is so hard and long-standing that it can't be solved overnight.

Time will be needed to normalize the situation, perhaps as much as 12 or 18 months.

The employee will strengthen his/her positions, overcome the past obstacles and prove his/her loyalty to the boss.

Money. Your financial positions will improve. The estimated dates of receiving the largest amounts of money are July 2, 3, 10, 11, 20, 21. But in early July, a large amount will be spent: perhaps you will have to lend money to a friend or pay for some service.

Love. Family. For you, July has an obvious professional orientation, so there will be no time left for personal life. But those who are engaged in a long-standing family quarrel will continue it.

There are complex real-estate related issues on the agenda again. But they will hardly be resolved this month.

Many families will also have problems with their children, and a lot of money will be required to solve those problems.

Relations with family members will be much better. Probably, the difficulties inside the family will be overcome.

Health. In July, your energy potential is high enough and you won't fall ill.

SCORPIO

This month, you can make erroneous assessments and judgments, so don't rush and don't make important decisions. Your time will come, though somewhat later!

Job. Career. Although the sky is obviously clearing up above you, the last month's problems are still relevant. In particular, relations with the colleagues from other cities and countries still make you feel uneasy, and you will have to face that once again in mid July.

In the first tenday period, there is a probability of a sudden conflict with some of your business partners, related to your common business, its direction and development.

Intrigues of your competitors are also possible in this period.

You should remain calm during this uneasy time. Don't be too angry or picky. Solve the problems calmly and step by step, and remember that you are on the right track.

In August, many in your entourage will also understand this. The same is important for the employees.

Money. Your financial positions will improve towards the end of July. The largest amounts of money can be expected from July 22 through July 26. Decent amounts can also be expected on July 13, 14.

Love. Family. Personal problems will persist. Relations with the relatives are still tense, more conflicts can be expected in mid July.

The good news is that relations with the children are changing for the better, and this will somewhat stabilize the family situation.

The lovers will understand that a bad peace is better than a good war, and begin correcting the mistakes, often successfully.

Health. This month, your energy potential will improve substantially, and even those who fell ill last month, will be getting much better.

But the stars still recommend you to be careful in mid July on trips and when driving. It would also be a bad idea to hit the road on the "black" days of the month, from July 8 through 14.

SAGITTARIUS

This won't be the most successful month, and all you need is just have it behind you using your past experience and the ability to take punch. Very soon, you will forget about the current problems and find yourself in the wonderful August sun.

Job. Career. July is better for personal life and rest, but if job is your priority, be ready to face numerous problems dating back to the past.

Disagreements with some of your business partners about financial matters continue. Perhaps you have to accept the inevitable expenses as well as the fact that you have to give something away.

In early July, there is also a possibility of unexpected problems with your colleagues from other cities or countries, caused by circumstances you can hardly change.

Don't worry, nothing too bad will happen: the problems that arose in June and July will be resolved successfully in August and September.

The employee can take a two-week vacation in July to work at home, inside his/her family.

Money. In terms of finance, July will not be very good. There will be permanent expenses, while the income will decrease substantially.

However, you can profit from real estate operations this month as well as from support of you parents or family members.

Negotiations about obtaining a credit will be successful, but you should read the documents attentively and negotiate carefully the proposed interest.

Love. Family. In the sphere of personal relations, much depends on the past as well as on your intentions and your partner's position.

The divorcing spouses may continue to quarrel over common property and home. This time, however, it will be necessary to take into account the partner's position and give him/her what they consider their own.

The friendly couples will overcome the numerous domestic and other difficulties together. A small renovation is also quite possible.

Relations with the partner's relatives will suddenly get worse. In early July, a serious conflict is possible. But in late July, everything will be clarified and the problems will disappear.

The lovers will experience cooling in their relationship. In another case, numerous problems will make them date less frequently.

Health. This month, your energy potential is not high, so take care of yourself and be reasonable.

In early July, be careful when traveling and driving

CAPRICORN

This month, you will have to deal with someone else's opinion, and it's highly probable that it will be opposite to yours. The above is equally true for work and for love.

Job. Career. This month, you will have to tackle numerous problems dating back to the past. There will be another showdown with your business partners or hostile competitors. Although this time they will be more polite than in the recent past, your opinions will still differ.

You and they will only come to terms if all of you understand that collaboration is mutually profitable. In one case, those are common interests related to your colleagues from other cities or countries, while in the other - mutual financial obligations.

Relations with the business partners from far away will be somewhat better, negotiations are possible, but they will be slightly delayed and at first fruitless. But even this seemingly useless dialogue can have its positive consequences, which will become clear later on.

Money. Your financial situation is unstable and, in one case, is related to your job, while in the other – to your personal life.

You will have a big and unexpected expenditure in early July.

Love. Family. For many representatives of your sign, the most important July events will happen at home, inside the family. The heaven will deliver a blow to the spouses whose relationship has long been hanging by a thread. In July, a very small thing, such as a reckless word, will be enough for you to explode. All what has accumulated will break through without a visible reason. It would have happened anyway, sooner or later, but the decisive moment is close.

The influence of the relatives can somewhat, though not completely, improve the situation.

In early July, you will face unexpected problems with the children; in many cases, those will result in big expenses.

For those in love, this month won't be easy. Some controversial issues are possible from July 7 through 12, but then the situation will improve and, a bit later, the problem will be solved.

Health. In July, your energy potential is not high. Besides, July's nervous and troublesome atmosphere can make you feel exhausted.

If this is the case, remember that health is the main thing, the rest depends on it, so act accordingly.

AQUARIUS

This month can hardly be called successful. Nothing extraordinary will happen, but this is not the right time for doing important things. Behave moderately and carefully, no matter what you do.

Job. Career. The last month's problems persist, and you need to analyze them.

Those who have legal problems or undergo auditing should analyze all the details of these complicated events.

The entrepreneurs and managers will put things in order in their team and perhaps shuffle the staff.

At the same time, work is going on as before, so you will be able to do a lot even in this difficult month. This is mainly routine work and preparation for new professional undertakings.

The complicated relations will some of your friends or high-position people will gradually normalize. This will happen in late July or in August.

The employee is recommended to do his/her job diligently, be modest and keep putting one foot in front of the other. This is important for all representatives of your sign, regardless of their occupation.

Money. Despite delays in business and other professional difficulties, there will be no financial problems. On the contrary, your will have more money this month, and, besides regular earnings, you can expect that you will pay off your old debts.

The estimated dates of getting the largest amounts are July 2, 3, 10–12, 20–24.

Love. Family. This month can hardly be called successful in terms of personal relations. In early July, there is a possibility of conflicts with your loved ones, as well as housing problems. It's hard to say what exactly will happen in this or that case, but there will definitely be a cause for concern.

Uranus, which has established itself firmly in the sky sector related to home or other real estate, warns you about changes in this area.

In particular, the loving spouses will plan to buy a new house/apartment, and those plans will come true.

The unamicable couples can come into conflict about the common real estate. Such quarrels can become regular.

In July, the lovers can't meet as often as they want. The couples that had a big quarrel last month will hardly find a way to reconciliation.

Health. In July, those who have old chronic diseases will face the urgent need to be treated.

Besides, some of your family members can fall ill; they will need your attention and compassion.

pisces

During this difficult month, you should rely on your intuition. It will help you take the right steps even in situations, absolutely new for you.

Job. Career. In July, your personal life may become more important for you than your job and career. But if you are fully focussed on your job, you must be ready for numerous difficulties that date back to the recent past. In particular, in the first half of the month, you will face problems with the old friends or high-position people who provided you with services and patronage some time ago.

Besides, from July 6 through 14, relations with your colleagues from other cities and countries will become complicated.

Pay close attention to those problems as they can happen again a bit later. In this difficult period, rely on yourself and your ability to find a way out of the most difficult situations. Remember that nothing but your efforts can lead to a good result.

The best time for doing your job is the last week of July, when you will be able to move your business several steps forward.

But in general, all your professional undertakings will go on very slowly, which relates equally to all representatives of your sign, regardless of their social status and occupation.

Money. Financially, July is mostly unsuccessful. There will be permanent expenditures, related to either business or personal life. In July, the income will be very low or maybe there will be none.

Love. Family. Your personal life will be rather controversial. The lovers who had a big quarrel last month can regret it. You will have enough time to think better and maybe take the first step. And even if not everything goes on smoothly and you think that there is next to no progress, don't be upset, act softly and politely. The world doesn't stand still. Make up for the time you have lost, and, in the long run, everything will be OK.

The parents will have problems with their children. Depending on the situation, those problems can look different. In any case, you can resolve many issues this month, especially if you act independently, without relying on anybody else.

Relations with some of the family members will become complicated; perhaps the reason will be an old debt or other obligations. A sudden quarrel will erupt in mid July. Normalizing the situation will require time; this may happen not earlier than in late August or in September.

Health. In July, your energy potential is rather high, but the stars recommend you to be cautious on trips and when driving.

In all respects, the traumatic time is the period from July 6 through 14, as well as 28 through 30.

AUGUST

ARIES

One way or another, the problems of the previous months are losing their severity. The last and most joyful summer month is ahead. It seems that you are going to have a well-deserved rest!

Job. Career. Those who keep working will do a lot. Complicated relations with colleagues from other cities or countries are getting calmer and more predictable. Although it's clear that this is a temporary situation, you should take advantage of it as such events don't happen very often! There is no one as experienced, smart and strong as you, so go ahead!

All trips scheduled for August will be very successful, as well as negotiations.

Creative people and diplomats of all levels will achieve the greatest success. You will become more popular. Besides, you will be able to look at many things from a different angle as well as get back to the battlefield stronger and with new ideas.

Money. In terms of finance, this month is not very good. There will be numerous expenses, often related to vacation as well as to the needs of your loved ones. For you, it will definitely be a pleasure to spend what you have earned, and that's right. Can anything be better?

On the other hand, August has some pleasant surprises and gifts in store for you. Serious amounts of money can be expected at the end of the month, from August 26 through 31.

Love. Family. This year, August seems to be made for love. Singles and those disappointed in previous attachments will have a great chance to have a bright affair. The romance will develop rapidly and can go far.

Many representatives of your sign will break free from the paws of the work problems to the bright sunshine and start doing what they want and have dreamed about.

The stable married people will spend time with their children. The latter will make them happy.

Health. This month, you are healthy, energetic and extremely attractive, which everyone you come across will notice.

Go to the numerous August parties and dress up.

TAURUS

In August, the comfort zone for you is your home, family and your loved ones. You will hardly be interested in anything else.

Job. Career. But the incorrigible workaholics can tackle what they have long being putting off "till better times". The stars also promise "green light" to the constructors and all those whose business is somehow related to real estate.

Towards the end of August, your ties will the colleagues from other cities and countries will become more active; a successful trip is likely. These are the old, time-proven ties, which can be useful both now and in the future. In this regard, the period from August 25 through 31 is especially good.

The complicated situations of the last months will temporarily lose their severity, but you should be on alert as the problem can arise again some time later.

Money. In terms of finance, August is rather calm. Many will profit from various real-estate operations, either selling or renting. Getting a credit on good terms is quite probable. Some of the representatives of your sign can count on their parents' support and even getting inheritance.

Love. Family. Unusual things will be happening in your personal life. Throughout the month, you will be irritated and impatient, which will result in heated debate. You will be defending your positions very undiplomatically, even rudely.

It's up to you of course, but this kind of behavior never leads to success. The family members will be trying to adjust to your whims, but in the long run they will have enough of that.

In one case, complex operations related to real estate will be involved, such as renovation, acquisition of furniture and other things of everyday importance. Perhaps your attitudes will be quite different, and this will result in conflicts.

In another, more complicated variant, you may be displeased with many things in your personal life. Your family members will understand that your revolutionary mood is not a whim. Time will show what is to be done, but there seems to be no way back.

Potentially, this is a situation when, as they say, 'the upper classes have no ability, while the lower classes have no wish.' Take this into account if you want to avoid this situation.

Things will be better towards the end of the month: perhaps, the quarrelling spouses will be temporarily united by the children.

Late August is also the best time for those in love. Their relationship will improve significantly, they may travel together and perhaps even have another honeymoon.

Health. This month, your energy potential is not high, you will often have states of lethargy and fatigue. The best cure for that is exercising and walking, as well as a cup of coffee in the morning.

The women are quite likely to be pregnant.

GEMINI

Throughout the month, you will feel optimistic and confident. But before hitting the road, check the route and see what is going on ahead of you!

Job. Career. In August, you will be defending your ideas and positions quite resolutely. Relations with the colleagues from other cities or countries will be more active; a successful trip is possible. Thanks to your efforts, the complicated relations with some of your business partners are getting better.

It seems that you have found some arguments and backed them up with facts, which your business partners have to take into account. On the other hand, you also benefit from these contacts. So, after a difficult period, the collaboration is rising to a higher level. Remember, though, that there is a possibility of some problems in the future.

This month is generally good for you, but some unforeseen and unexpected obstacles are possible. The stars recommend you to put the documents in order, keep an eye on the details, and never stop monitoring the incoming information.

Also, try not to break the law or use controversial paths this month.

Money. The financial situation is calm. It seems that you managed to solve many problems last month and leave the most painful issues behind.

You can count on some money in late August, but it will hardly be related to your primary job: it's either a credit or an old debt returned to you, or maybe "a little help from your friends."

Love. Family. Your personal relations are getting better, too. The spouses and lovers who had a big quarrel in the past, will resume their relationship. Perhaps they will travel together, and this will help them strengthen their relations.

However, the problem can arise again in the nearest future, so take advantage of the temporary improvement to become as close to each other as possible.

Discuss the topics of mutual importance as there is a chance to be understood. This relates both to the spouses and the lovers.

In late August, the agenda will include various issues related to your home. Everything will be OK in this area and you will avoid conflicts.

Health. This month, you are healthy, energetic and enterprising. But the stars strongly recommend you to be cautious on trips and when driving. The first days of August are especially dangerous in this regard.

CANCER

You are in for a reward in August. You have been working hard, and it's time to enjoy the results.

Job. Career. Although August, the last summer month, is traditionally the time of entertainment and rest, you will spend it working hard, which you like, though.

The entrepreneurs and managers will solve many problems of the past and start moving towards a better future. Besides, you can count on striking profitable deals, getting a profit for the previous work, and having good luck in your current business.

The employee will come to terms with his/her colleagues, and the boss – with his/her subordinates.

The generally good picture of the month will be marred by your relations with some of your friends or business partners; financial claims will be involved. It's up to you to decide what to do in this situation.

Perhaps the demands placed on you will be unfair and need an additional discussion.

Money. But in general, August is good financially. You will be getting money on a regular basis, and its amount will increase substantially. The estimated dates of getting the largest amounts are August 1, 2, 9–11, 20, 21, 28–30.

Love. Family. For the personal life, the best time is late August. In this period, the divorcing couples will be able to discuss the most sensitive topics and reach a mutually acceptable compromise. It is not excluded that the relatives will act as mediators and make a highly positive influence on your partner.

Towards the end of August, the loving spouses, just as most of the lovers, will be able to travel together, and their relationship will improve a lot.

Health. August is good for various health-improving events.

Sports, massage, a trip to a resort or sanatorium are quite likely in the second half of August or in early September.

LEO

August is good for solving many controversial issues both in business and in personal life. You are quite ready to move mountains, so go ahead!

Job. Career. You don't think anymore that the problems of the previous months can't be solved. You are moving step by step, coping with intrigues, audits, and just everything life uses for testing your strength.

Besides solving the old problems, you will be able to take a step forward towards important changes. In the first half of the month, you will have to face various, sometimes unpleasant circumstances, but in late August, you will celebrate victory.

The entrepreneurs and the managers will succeed in solving difficult tasks related to new business trends, while the employees will overcome the lack of understanding on the part of the boss.

Confidence will help all representatives of your sign, despite the occupation, solve the tasks you have never faced before.

Money. Towards the end of the month, the financial situation will improve a lot.

The estimated dates of getting the largest amounts of money are August 26 through 31.

Love. Family. For the personal life, August is even more successful than for the career. Many representatives of your sign will be able to combine business with pleasure: they will work hard and then have a good rest.

The married people will spend much time with their children; the latter will bring them a lot of joy.

The lovers will have a great opportunity to become closer to each other; perhaps the will travel together.

The singles will probably meet an interesting person and have a long and passionate affair.

Many families will have new children or grandchildren. Take advantage of the stars' location – plunge into new relationships and strengthen the existing ones!

Health. This month, your energy potential is high enough and you will stay healthy.

VIRGO

In August, your main task is achieving inner balance and harmony. Your loved ones and, of course, your family will help you reach the goal.

Job. Career. In August, many representatives of your sign will relax or do their housework. This will be a good decision since you are not likely to have any big achievements in business, while you definitely need some rest.

But those who can't do without working, will be able to hold some organizational events to strengthen their business.

The most successful of you will be the constructors and all those whose business has something to do with real estate.

The best time for the representatives of other professions is the last week of August. In this period, your business partners from other cities and countries will be very active. Productive negotiations and a successful business trip are possible.

Money. The financial situation is stable, but it's not about your own funds. The money may come from successful operations with real estate; also possible are financial support from your business partners and a business loan. Some of the representatives of your sign can count on the help from their parents, the spouse or a loved one.

Love. Family. Many will spend the last summer month relaxing or doing their housework. It is possible that you will finalize a big renovation, sell some property, or buy something for your home.

Relations with the children will be quite harmonious this month. In August, especially in the last week of the month, you will meet with your family members and relatives living in other cities or countries. The lovers and the young married couples can count on support from their parents, which will help you buy a home.

The couples that used to have problems in the past will live peacefully in August. The peace will let you resolve moral and financial claims without any conflicts.

Health. In August, your energy potential is not high, so if you want to relax lying on a sofa reading a book, don't hesitate to do it! In August, you will start gaining weight, so eat healthy food, walk, and, of course, do sports.

LIBRA

This month, you can kill not two but a dozen birds with one stone! So set the goals and go forward!

Job. Career. In August, the main tendency is improvement of relations with your colleagues from other cities and countries. Recent conflicts are getting calmer, and you have possibilities for fruitful collaboration.

Presently, you are supported by people who have a high social standing. They will help you in your numerous undertakings, and their support will be timely and effective.

Towards the end of the month, many controversial issues will be resolved related to land, real estate or other large property. Don't waste time and use these opportunities!

In August, you will also be able to engage in collaboration your old business partners and new ones. Your friends will make the difference if you ask them to help you and work together with you. Be sure that they won't refuse!

Your eloquence and charm promise all kinds of victories. Thanks to your confidence, you will succeed in solving all the tasks. Trips scheduled for August will be very successful.

The only minus of the month will be disagreements with your friends or some high-position people. Those disagreements can be rather unexpected and have a financial nature. The situation will get back to normal in late August or in September, when you will finally reach agreement.

Money. Except that unpleasant episode, your financial situation is stable, but not more than that. You can't expect any big income this month; towards the end of the month, you can expect a real-estate profit. In August, you will probably spend much money for your vacation, family and children.

Love. Family. Many representatives of your sign will combine business with pleasure – they will work had and have a good rest. There is a chance of a good trip, meeting your old friends as well as some of your well-disposed relatives.

Relations inside the family are harmonious. Towards the end of August, many will move to another house or apartment. The divorcing couples will finally solve the painful property division issue.

The singles can count on making new friends as well as on a bright romance. This is likely to happen on a trip or when meeting with people who have arrived from far away.

Health. In August, your energy potential is rather high, so you will stay healthy. This month is good for experimenting with your image – from changing the hairstyle and buying new clothes to plastic surgery.

SCORPIO

You will be extremely energetic and ambitious throughout the month, which means that you will definitely reach your goals!

Job. Career. This month, you will have a great opportunity to show all your best qualities. A promotion is possible, as well as approval of your work by those whose opinion is very important for you. Thanks to all this and to your luck, you will move things forward and get a chance to beat your competitors.

Complicated relations with some of your partners can result in conflicts in the first half of the month, but currently, the ball is in your court, and you are the only person to decide what way the business will go. But the stars predict that after the mutual attacks, the parties will find an acceptable compromise. The situation can get back to normal in the third tenday period of August or in the first half of September.

In the last week of the month, your relations with the colleagues living in other cities and countries will become more active; a successful business trip is possible. The old ties will be restored as well as the former collaboration. The employee can be promoted or get a job offer from another organization.

Money. Financially, August is one of the best months in 2019. Money will be coming on a regular basis, its amount will grow substantially. The entrepreneur can expect profitable contracts, while the employee can have a salary rise or a bonus. The estimated dates of getting the highest amounts are August 1, 2, 9,10, 20.

Love. Family. Professionally active representatives of this sign will have next to no time for private life: job is their main priority.

As to the romantic representatives of this highly emotional sign, the stars recommend to those who can't live without love to be more careful with their loved ones. Unexpectedly, your partner can start being aggressive, which will result in conflicts in the first half of the month. Towards the end of August, the situation will normalize, maybe because your older relatives will act as mediators.

In the third tenday period, there is a chance of meetings with friends, ex- partners, and relatives living in other cities or countries; a successful trip is possible.

Health. In August, you are at the peak of life activity and will stay healthy. This is also a good time for doing sports or maybe dancing. In a word, use your energy, and everything will be just great!

SAGITTARIUS

This month, you will have to act as the leader, and you will do it well, there is no doubt about it. Do what you think is right - this will open many doors for you!

Job. Career. This month, many representatives of your sign will find new ways of making money. It's probable that your business partners from other cities or countries will help you and you will have a successful business trip. The first half of the month can bring you unexpected organizational problems, which you will overcome in the second half. One of the most successful periods in business will begin, almost everything will go one well.

The entrepreneur will rise to a higher level and strike profitable deals, while the employee can expect a promotion or a job offer from another organization. In a word, you are going to have a dynamic and positive time, when you can move far ahead in any undertaking.

Money. Your financial situation will improve significantly in the third tenday period of August, and this positive process will continue in September. The estimated dates for getting the largest amounts are August 3, 4, 12, 13, 21, 26-30.

Love. Family. Your romantic life will also be very interesting. Those in love can travel together and have a very good time. The stars advise you to schedule the trip for the second half of August, which is the best time for traveling.

Mind that unpleasant surprises are possible on the road in the first half of the month. This is also important for those who are planning a business trip.

The singles and those disappointed in their previous affections can count on an office romance, which can begin unexpectedly on a business trip or at a new working place.

Health. This month, your energy potential is quite high and you will stay healthy.

CAPRICORN

You are in for a surprisingly peaceful period of time. You can restore harmony in a relationship or in your own soul and do what you always wanted - that is, just enjoy living.

Job. Career. August is not very good for a professional activity. The best thing you can now do is to put your things in order, finalize the work started earlier, and prepare the ground for the forthcoming achievements. They will definitely happen this year and continue in 2020.

But August can be very successful for the constructors and those whose business has something to do with real estate.

The last tenday period of August is good for renewing relations with the colleagues from other cities and countries. There is a chance of a successful business trip, renewal of old projects on a new, modern basis.

Money. In terms of finance, August can be rather uneven. In the first half of the month, a lot of money will be spent for the family needs. These include renovation in the new house as well as solving the children's problems.

The second half of the month won't be so ruinous, but it will be also less successful.

Love. Family. For many representatives of your sign, the main events will happen at home and inside the family.

The friendly couples will keep renovating their city house, apartment, or summer house. In some cases, this will happen far from home.

In many families, problems with the children are possible, depending on the previous situations. But practically always, they will require substantial expenses.

The divorcing couples will solve the property division issues, but can have a conflict concerning their children's future.

This month is not very good for the lovers. In its first half, it will be clear that there is a connection between love and money. But if you have emotional pleasure, the price doesn't matter. So decide which is more important for you, and everything will be OK.

In late August, the lovers and the spouses can go on trips and have a great time.

They will probably travel to the places they know well, but they will be able to find something new there and thus won't be disappointed.

Health. In August, especially in its first and second tenday periods, your energy potential is not high, so take care and be reasonable. Your main task in August is to have a good rest and become strong enough for a breakthrough in your career, expected in fall.

AQUARIUS

It is going to be a very active, a bit chaotic, but, in general, a very positive month. You will be smart, original and witty, which everyone you come across will notice.

Job. Career. In August, the main thing will be activization of your ties with the friends and people having high social positions. Communicating with them will be both pleasant and useful. You will even have new business perspectives.

Don't be afraid to express your wishes and ideas! You will be understood correctly.

At the same time, conflicts with the business partners are possible in the first tenday period of August. The reason will be a controversial property issue.

In many cases, this will happen rather unexpectedly, but after heated debate, a mutually acceptable solution will be found.

In this regard, the last tenday period of August and the first half of September are the best.

Money. In terms of finance, August is rather neutral. There will be no big income, while the expenditures will be predictable and reasonable.

In late August or in September, a property related income is possible.

Love. Family. In many cases, the main August events can happen at home and inside the family. The loving spouses will be solving difficult problems related to real estate, and each will have his/her own opinion on this troubling topic.

Mind that some of your loved ones won't be very sensitive and tactful. Don't take it to heart, do calmly what you think to be right, but don't ignore your loved ones' opinions. Controversy, as you know, sometimes serves the cause of truth.

The unfriendly couples will suddenly begin talking about divorce and even about dividing property, first of all home. But in the long run, this will turn out to be not serious, and the situation will get back to normal in late August.

The singles and those disappointed in previous affections can count on finding new, interesting friends.

Romantic emotions and events are possible throughout the month. Go to the numerous August parties and dress up, the more so that you are charming and witty.

The lovers may have problems with their parents, but in the long run, the obstacles will be overcome.

Health. A slight weakening of the energy potential will be felt in the last week of August, but it will hardly result in a serious illness.

pisces

This hot summer month will be extremely successful for you. Set the main goals and don't allow the circumstances to distract you. The result won't keep you waiting.

Job. Career. From the professional point of view, this month will be quite good. The entrepreneurs can count on profitable and promising contracts.

August is very good for communicating with your boss, with all kinds of official authorities, and with auditors.

However, despite the general improvements, some problems are possible. In particular, sudden complications in relations with the colleagues living in other cities and countries are likely in the first tenday period. You will only be able to overcome these obstacles in late August. This is the time when you will come to terms and continue your collaboration.

The end of the month is good for restoring the old ties, meetings with your old friends as well as with high-position persons, who provided you with services and patronage. Appearance of new people is also probable in this period.

In August, the employee can count on an additional assignment and good dividends. He/she can be promoted or get a job offer from another company.

Money. The financial situation will be much better as a result of an overall improvement of your business. The estimated dates of getting large amounts of money are August 1, 2, 9, 10, 18, 19, 28, 29.

There will be little expenses, and all of them will be predictable and reasonable.

Love. Family. For the personal life, the best period is the last ten days of August, when the planets of love and passion, Mars and Venus, unite happily in your sector of the sky responsible for the relationship. This means that the feelings of the experienced lovers will break out with renewed vigor, while the lonely people can expect a bright romance.

Almost all representatives of your sign, for whom *love* is a very important word, will experience a surge of emotions.

In the first half of the month, there is a possibility of problems with the relatives, whose attitude will be somewhat unexpected for you.

But towards the end of August, all problems will be resolved, and the situation will get back to normal.

Health. This month, you will work a lot, and your body may fail you from time to time. To avoid this, you must have a good rest. And don't forget about health-improving procedures.

SEPTEMBER

ARIES

Vacations are over, working days are ahead. The planets have opened a new chapter in your life book.

Job. Career. September is quite good for working. You will have a lot of work: you are laying, with your own hands, the foundation of another important business.

Everything will depend on you, things will go on well. But you will have some problems in the first half of the month; to solve them, your time and efforts will be required.

Relations with the colleagues from other cities and countries are getting worse, and you don't want it to happen again. But you have enough experience pushing your business forward while staying between the devil and the deep sea.

This time, it will be the case, too. Thanks to your effort and ability to find solutions in the most complicated situations, the problem will move from the dead point. Perhaps your supporters and allies will help you. Late September as well as October are especially important in this regard.

Those having legal problems will also face some difficulties, which will be overcome next month.

The employee will be doing his/her job diligently and have the boss's appreciation and respect. But there is a possibility of having problems with some of the colleagues, and the stars strongly advise you to stay away from intrigue. There can be new people in the team, which will create anxiety and fuss.

Money. Your financial situation will be much better, money will be coming on a regular basis, and its amount will grow substantially.

The estimated dates of getting the largest amounts are September 8, 9, 18, 19, 26, 27.

There will be a few expenses, all predictable and reasonable.

Love. Family. This month, your personal life will be less important for you than your job. The only exception is those who have office romances: they will be solving work tasks together, and this will make them still closer to each other.

Many families will face problems with their relatives; most likely those will be the partner's relatives. Perhaps you have experienced something like this before, so there will be nothing new for you in this situation.

Health. In September, you will have a lot of responsibilities, both at home and at work.

But you should try to relax from time to time. Remember that "a healthy body equals a healthy mind."

TAURUS

What can be better and more interesting that leaving the past behind and beginning everything from scratch? Life will raise the veil of a new future for you. This perspective

*attracts and scares you at the same time. But in just 6
months you will understand that you are on the right track.*

Job. Career. The best September achievement will be better relations
with your colleagues from other cities and countries. You will get in touch
with your former business partners and old friends as well make new
acquaintances and maybe have a successful business trip.

Many representatives of your sign will resume old projects, though on a
more solid foundation.

At the same time, relations with some of your business partners or high-
position people will become difficult again. The reason can be financial
claims, and the odd and contradictory attitude of your opponents will
result in misunderstandings and conflicts. You have come across this kind
of things more than once, so this time, it will be nothing new for you.

Money. In September, your financial situation is rather unstable. All
kinds of expenditures are likely. Some of you will be "ruined" by their
professional undertakings, others will spend a lot of money for the needs
of their families, children, and loved ones.

Love. Family. For many representatives of your sign, the main events will
happen at home and inside the family. You will want to spend time the
way you have always dreamed about, for example, visit your old friends
or relatives living far away.

The children will, in general, make you happy, although their training,
education and other activities are still expensive. But you are ready for
that because - who, if not you?

This month is also not bad for the lovers, especially if they stop counting
the money and travel together. Listen to your soul rather than mind, and
everything will be OK.

The stars are telling you not to introduce anyone to your family and love affairs, even the closest friends. Sometimes you can tell people your secrets, but this is not the case.

By the way, these recommendations are also relevant for doing business.

September will bring you new acquaintances, and the singles will have a great chance to meet someone who will make their life better.

Health. This month, your energy potential is rather high and you will stay healthy.

GEMINI

For you, September is the time of serious changes in your everyday life and lifestyle. You will have to cover your bases!

Job. Career. Professionally, September is not very good, the exception being the constructors and those whose business is related to land and real estate – the stars will ensure "green lite" for those people's business and finance.

The others can take a leave and focus on their personal affairs. But if you have to work, the best idea would be to put things in order in the office and other premises as well as analyze the state of the arts in your business and clear the field for new undertakings.

Relations with some of your business partners will become difficult, old claims and grievances will be revived once again.

Perhaps the reason will be the difference in the views on the business and its further development, but, in a more difficult version, even its division. Most likely, the last word will be pronounced, and it will be very sharp.

The employee who keeps working is recommended to be more attentive to his/her duties to avoid the boss's anger.

Money. In terms of finance, September is rather neutral. But you can make money on real-estate operations as well as get financial support from your parents and the older family members.

The entrepreneur may solve successfully a controversial issue related to real estate or other large property.

Love. Family. For many representatives of your sign, the main events will take place at home and inside the family. It's quite possible that you will decide to start renovation or reconstruction, and this decision will be successful.

But due to those troublesome events, the atmosphere in some families will be tense. Even the loving spouses can quarrel periodically, and then put up.

The unfriendly couples as well as those who decided to get divorced are recommended to start dividing the property and, first of all, the home.

Efficient housewives should remember that guests will be visiting your home more often than usual, or relatives will unexpectedly come over.

In other words, your home will be checked for strength in different ways, and it's up to you to turn it into a fortress before the forthcoming onslaught of problems. Besides, you should determine your relations with the loved ones.

Health. This month, your energy potential is not high, so try to sleep well and don't eat and drink too much.

CANCER

This month, you can make important decisions that will determine your life for years to come. Now you are at the peak of your intellectual capabilities!

Job. Career. September is the month of movement and change. Contacts with your business partners from other cities or countries will be activated, a successful business trip is possible.

Many of you will resume relations with their old colleagues and take on an almost forgotten project. It will be successful if you can put it on a modern platform.

Besides, in September, you will meet new, interesting and somewhat unusual people. A little later, these relations can lead to fruitful collaboration and friendship.

At the same time, you will face old troubles. In one case, those will be legal problems, though in an acute form this time. In another, a hostile colleague, also living far way, will make new claims or behave badly. But you have come across such problems more than once, so this is nothing new for you.

The employee will face problems inside the team again; machinations of one of the colleagues are possible. This is a short-time problem, which will disappear towards the end of September.

Money. The financial situation is rather calm in September. Big income is not likely, but there will be no losses either. Those who have old debts are likely to start paying them off.

Love. Family. Your personal life will normalize somehow. Which is rather strange, because it seemed that after the recent violent conflicts, there was no way back. But many representatives of your sign find it hard to part with the past, which will be the case this time.

Ways to reconciliation will be found, and your severe partner will give up without a fight. In one case, a relative will act as an intermediary and peacemaker, in another, it will be the children. Others will decide not to divide their property.

The lovers and the spouses can travel together. This will reconcile them with each other and with life itself.

This month is also good for the singles. They can resume a relationship with someone from the past, as well as make many new acquaintances.

September is ideal for studying and gaining new knowledge. So go ahead to face the unknown.

Health. This month, you are active, witty and quite healthy. In the first half of September, however, the stars recommend you to be cautious when traveling or driving.

LEO

This month, you will have two components of success – passion and motivation. Good luck!

Job. Career. Professionally and financially, September is one of the best months of the year. This is a good time for making business agreements, working on the projects, as well as meeting potential employers. You will manage to make old plans and projects a reality and bring your colleagues and supporters to your business. Perhaps you will be able to revive an old project and put it on a new foundation.

The employee will improve his/her positions or get an interesting job offer.

Towards the end of the month, contacts with the colleagues from other cities and countries will become more active; there is a high probability of a business trip.

Money. Your financial situation will improve significantly as a result of the huge job you have done.

Old debts will be paid off to many of you, and, at the same time, you will be able to pay off yours.

This month's expenses will be mainly related to your children and loved ones; it is possible that you will have to spend more money than planned.

The estimated dates of getting the highest amounts are September 1, 7–9, 17–19, 26, 27.

Love. Family. In your personal life, there will be contradictory tendencies. The married people will be solving their children's problems and spend the lion's share of their budget. However, the stars warn the most caring representatives of your sign that the expenses can be excessive and not correspond to the real needs.

The lovers can have certain disagreements due to the different views on life and different value systems. In another case, money and unwillingness to spend it will be the reason of conflicts.

It's bad if love and money are interrelated, but this does happen sometimes. If this is the case with you, just decide what is more important to you and act accordingly. As to the stars, they believe that this is love indeed!

Health. In September, your energy potential is not very high, but you can definitely change your lifestyle and make it healthier; for example, go in for sports and have a healthy diet.

VIRGO

Perseverance, confidence and a non-standard approach to all issues will open up many doors for you. Though not all of them, unfortunately...

Job. Career. Throughout the month, you will be resolutely defending your ideas and positions. If this is the case, here is what the astrologer advises you: In the disputes, provide serious arguments and support them with facts. Also, make what you say quite comprehensible. This is very important, because a conflict with your business partners or opponents can happen again.

Perhaps you will face an ambiguous position of some of your colleagues, or simply deceit. This time, the reason can be disputed property, finance, or different views on the future of your business. However, you have a strong position and will be able to defend your legitimate rights.

In September, contacts with your colleagues from other cities and countries will become stronger and more active. You will also make new friends.

They can support your ideas and, subsequently, become your efficient business partner.

It is possible that the employee will be searching for another application of his/her talents, and there will definitely be some progress in this direction.

Business trips scheduled for this month will be quite successful.

Money. In terms of finance, the last week of the month will be the most successful one. You will definitely get a large amount of money between September 27 and 30.

Love. Family. Those whose priority is their personal life, should expect various events to happen in September.

In many families, problems with real estate will persist, so even the loving couples will experience some tension.

In some cases, the problem will be a home for the children, and the reality will be worse than the dreams.

The quarrelling couples will keep dividing the property, but the problem is going to be solved soon.

The lovers will live this month in rather a friendly way, but many of them will have to overcome resistance of the dissatisfied parents.

September is good for restoring old relationships and making new friends.

Trips scheduled for this month will be very successful and distract you from numerous problems.

Health. In September, you will be supported by Mars, Mercury, Sun, and Venus, which means that you will have a lot of energy. The stars strongly recommend you to use it properly, and everything will be OK!

LIBRA

Intuition will help you make the right steps in various situations you will find yourself in this month. Towards its end, you will have something to celebrate!

Job. Career. In September, you will face again numerous problems that have been growing in your entourage since long go. There will be difficulties in your relations with the colleagues from other cities or countries. Some of the foreign partners will be hampering your business the way they did before. The reason of the conflicts will be real estate, land, documents, or large property. A lot of effort will be required so that you would defend your rights.

But despite of the problems, your business is going on well. As the old saying goes, "The dogs may bark, but the caravan moves on." You will reach your goal anyway, which is the most important thing. A bit later, everyone will accept this.

The managers and the self-employed are still recommended to be very attentive to their subordinates: they are rather vulnerable in this sphere, which can result in serious problems.

The employees should be more careful with their colleagues as the old intrigue, rumors and gossip may continue.

Money. Your financial situation is rather stable. There is a chance of additional incomes related to real estate, and getting a loan; support by the business partners or a loved one are also possible.

You can also get an inheritance.

Love. Family. In personal life, you will have to be very patient and tactful, and act diplomatically.

Perhaps, it will again be about property division, and the divorcing couples may fail to come to terms. Relations with the relatives will suddenly become complicated, and they will stir the pot.

But this time, you will manage to reach your goal. You will keep what, in your opinion, belongs to you.

The loving spouses will finalize the renovation and even set a moving date, while the quarrelling ones will get separated at last.

Health. This month, your energy potential is not high, so lead a healthy lifestyle and take care of yourself in every possible way.

Besides, you should be careful when traveling and driving. The probability of unpleasant events is rather high this month.

SCORPIO

Throughout the month, you will be extremely energetic and ambitious, which will bring fruit – you will be noticed and appreciated.

Job. Career. This month, the main tendency will be finding new ties. The old ones will be improved. You can make new friends, too. Many will contact colleagues from other cities or countries. A successful business trip is possible.

In September, your friends and people with a high social position will take an active part in your business. Their impact on your business will be absolutely positive.

Many representatives of your sign will become popular and needed, which will influence positively your reputation and business.

Despite the obvious success, you should be more prudent and not take on serious obligations, especially financial ones.

Set your goals and follow them without backing off. In general, your business is OK, but this is not the right time for daydreaming.

Money. In terms of finance, September will be uneven. Your income will hardly decrease, but the expenses will increase significantly. In one case, they are related to business, while in the other, to the family, children and loved ones.

Love. Family. In your personal life, usual things will be happening. Your romance requires not only moral effort, but also a lot of money. Besides, you can't be sure that your partner is quite sincere and honest with you. It is bad if love and money are interrelated, and if this is the case, think twice whether you should keep this relationship.

Many representatives of your sign will have to choose between the old and new affections. It is possible that you will have to sit between two chairs for a while.

Contacts with the relatives will become much more active; perhaps you will meet with those of them who live in another city or country.

Many families will have problems with the children, which will result in large expenses. The stars advise you to control the older ones as well as make sure that the younger ones are feeling well. This will help you smooth out most of the problems quite probable in September.

Health. This month, your energy potential is rather high and you will stay healthy.

SAGITTARIUS

This month, you will open the door to a better future. This is what you have always dreamed about, so don't hesitate to go forward!

Job. Career. In terms of profession, September is one of the best months of the year. You will have a golden opportunity to show your talents in full splendor, and there is no doubt that you won't miss that chance. In particular, the entrepreneurs and managers will conclude large-scale, promising and very profitable deals.

The employee will have an amazing promotion opportunity; in one case, this will happen at the current organization, while in the other, at a larger one.

You are very talented and can do a lot, so aim at the highest standards!

All this has not been in demand for a long time, but now it's your finest hour! So roll up your sleeves and get straight to the point!

One advice: Despite the good luck, don't rest on your laurels, always come to terms with your business partners and employers, and don't be arrogant.

Money. In terms of finance, this month is not bad at all. You will be getting money on a regular basis, and its amount will grow significantly. The estimated dates of getting the largest amounts are September 3, 4, 7–9, 17–19, 24–27.

Love. Family. In your personal life, things won't be as good as at work. In all the families, relations will be far from ideal, and even the loving spouses may experience a certain cooling.

If you are too busy and can't pay much attention to your partner, just explain that to him/her. You are working not only for yourself, but also for your loved ones, and all family members are supposed to understand this.

Many families will face property-related problems. In one case, the conflict will be caused by the divorce and property division, while in the other, by a complicated situation which involves your home or summer house.

It's hard to say something definite about the lovers, because in September, the main events will be happening at work.

Health. This month, you are very strong and energetic and healthy.

CAPRICORN

Doing business energetically always brings excellent fruit. That's exactly what is going on now: you are moving forward overcoming all barriers.

Job. Career. In September, you will open the door to a better future, but it will be a "long and winding road." Sometimes, life is like the old Russian fairy tale: making your way through a terrible forest, you finally come to a beautiful meadow and find the scarlet flower of your dream. Your life is like that fairy tale: you will have to overcome a lot of obstacles to reach the goal.

Those who have ties with colleagues living in other cities and countries will face numerous problems.

Obstacles of an objective nature are possible, when moving to the goal will be hampered by law or some international events. Another option is uncertainty and unstable position of the foreign colleagues.

Towards the end of the month, many problems will be resolved and you will move on safely.

Those who have legal issues will face more obstacles, but towards the end of September, they will find the right way of overcoming them.

Money. Financially, this month is rather neutral. There will be no big income or loss. The expenses are predictable and reasonable.

Love. Family. In your personal life, everything is not simple. Many families will have conflicts with the relatives, but there will be nothing unexpected here. You have come across all that more than once and are quite ready for what is going to happen this time. The situation will remain the same, so make a decision and act accordingly.

For the lovers, the month will not be bad. You can travel together and have a great time. But those who are sitting between two chairs should be careful – this month, all secrets will be revealed.

The spouses will live this month without having much fun as well as without trials and tribulations. It's quite probable that some activities related to housing will be over one way or another, and now you want to go on vacation. Most couples will be able to do this.

Health. In September, you are quite healthy, but the stars strongly recommend you to be more attentive when traveling and driving. The probability of unpleasant events is rather high this month.

AQUARIUS

The stars recommend you to stay calm in September and not overestimate your abilities. Cover your bases!

Job. Career. September is not good for professional undertakings. There is a possibility of financial disagreements with some of your friends or high-position people. You have faced such problems more than once, so you understand very well what it's all about. But this time, the situation will be more controversial and acute, especially in the first half of September.

Towards the end of the month, the situation will improve, and get back to normal in October.

This is the case with the self-employed. The employee is recommended to do his/her job diligently, not come up with bold initiatives, and, if possible, not make the boss angry.

It's possible that you will have a two-week vacation and pay close attention to your private life.

Money. Financially, September will be very complicated. Your frequent expenses will be related either to business or to your personal life.

Those working in the area of finance, such as accountants, brokers, cashiers, or bankers, should be very cautious. Financial losses are quite probable this month.

In September, you can raise some money through real estate operations.

Love. Family. For many representatives of this sign, the main September events can take place at home and inside the family.

Some will start renovation, improve the interior and decorate the house. In a more large-scale variant, you will think of a new home and start moving in that direction.

The lovers will have a serious conversation (almost an ultimatum) about the future of the relationship, and a positive decision is unlikely. It only depends on you if it's a temporary situation or your romance is over. In any case, don't discuss any topics that have potential pitfalls – now it's not your time at all.

Health. This month, your energy potential is not high, so take care and make sure that you eat good food. Poisoning and intestine problems are quite probable this month.

pisces

Mind that some people in your entourage are not friendly and that many pursue their own goals. But there are those who can really help you.

Job. Career. In terms of professional activity, September is rather complicated. Your opponents as well as business partners will try, more than once, to confuse you and impose their rules of the game. The reason of the conflict is different views on the development of the business, and, in the worst-case scenario, its division.

All September situations will look like those you have faced before, so there is nothing new now. And although the competitors' claims are becoming still stronger, you can defend your positions. Help will come from your old friends and some high-position people, as well from the stars, which have a good position in the sky.

Using this help, you can retain your positions and defend your rights.

The employee will face serious competition, and he/she should remember that any mistake can result in worse relations with the boss. Be focused and concentrated, and, if required, don't ask your boss for help, but contact some of your older friends who occupy a good position at the organization. This will be the best decision.

Your relations with the colleagues from other cities and countries are going on well; you can have new business partners and friends.

Money. The financial situation is more or less neutral. There won't be much success in this area, but no losses either.

Love. Family. Your personal life will be very active this month. The spouses and the lovers will quarrel, put up, and then quarrel again. There will be numerous reasons for the conflicts. Some of you have different views on the future of the relationship and everyday problems, others defend vigorously their opinion, etc.

In any case, the stars advise you to try and accept the partner's point of view in order to avoid many problems.

In all matters, both professional and romantic, you can count on your old friends' compassion and support, they are always there to help you.

The singles can expect someone's close attention to them, and a sudden bright affair.

Many will have interesting opportunities in their personal life in faraway places. You can make new friends there as well as find new admirers. In some cases, a trip will be involved.

Health. This month, your energy potential is not very high, so lead a healthy life style and be moderate.

OCTOBER

ARIES

The main trends of this month are challenges and competition. Not the best situation, of course, but it won't let you feel bored. That's the kind of person you are!

Job. Career. It's hard to call October a successful month. You will have to spend most of the time defending your interests from the business partners and competitors. The reason is different views on the future of the business, and the desire to divide it. Nothing special, but you will have to fight for your place in the sun.

However, there are positive tendencies, too. For example, relations with the colleagues from other cities and countries are getting better; a successful business trip is possible. There won't be full understanding, but positive changes will definitely take place.

The employee's positions are not quite stable, that's why he/she must take into account other opinions, not make the boss angry, and be careful and moderate.

Money. The financial situation is rather contradictory this month.

This will be especially obvious towards the end of the month, when you will have a sudden and large expense.

In one case, this can be a result of misunderstandings with your colleagues or business partners, in the other, it can be related to the needs of your loved ones. Household related expenses are also possible.

In October, your income will be rather modest, but on October 15-17, 20-21, you can expect some money.

Love. Family. In your personal life, you will have to face your loved one's unusual activity. It can be followed by irritation or even aggression. In this case, the main thing is not to retaliate before listening patiently to your loved one.

This is what the stars advise you. Otherwise, you can drown in never-ending disputes, without any hope that "controversy will serve the cause of truth." This is equally important for the lovers and the spouses.

Many couples will have to spend time deciding how to use the family budget. In this case, don't be too demanding and principled. Take a step back, and everything will be OK.

Trips scheduled for October can be rather successful and even help you normalize the relationship.

Health. This month, your energy potential is not high, and the stars strongly recommend you to lead a healthy lifestyle and take care of yourself in all ways possible.

TAURUS

This month, you should be a modest Cinderella. The time to be a princess has not come yet!

Job. Career. October is a month full of all kinds of matters and obligations.

You are accustomed to your job as well as to the fact that it can bring not only joy, but also problems. The latter include worsening of the relations with the colleagues from other cities and countries, which seems strange after the last year's idyll. The situation can improve towards the end of the month, but a powerful stream of energy in that direction can only be expected in January-February 2020.

Relations with some of your business partners can become another stumbling block, but the reason maybe you: you don't want to accept your colleagues' position and listen to them. It's up to you, of course, but the revolutionary mood, which many representatives of your sign have, can bring about numerous problems. It mainly relates to the Taurus born in the first tenday period of the month.

The entrepreneurs and the managers are recommended to get ready for auditing, which can happen in October.

The employee can get additional assignments, but, most likely, the compensation will be good. Also possible are negotiations about a new job.

Money. Your financial situation will be better, but not fully stable. You will keep making big business-related investments and paying off the old debts. Many will have to finalize complex renovation, which also costs quite a pretty penny.

Love. Family. Most of October is absolutely business-oriented, so you will have too little time and energy left for private life.

This, or something else, can be the reason of family conflicts. Try to understand your loved ones, take into account their interests, especially if you are not planning big changes. These recommendations are also relevant for most lovers.

In many families, relations with the relatives will become worse. In all probability, it will be about the old debts or other obligations. Everything will get back to normal over time, but you should remember that your relatives' characters are changing, and, as the astrologer thinks, not for the better.

Cancel al trips this month as they will bring nothing but problems.

Health. This month, your energy potential is not high, so, despite being busy, try to find time for taking care of your body and for its natural needs - rest and sleep. October is good for massage, beauty treatments, and just walking. The drivers are advised to be cautious when driving.

GEMINI

October is cheerful, though a bit ruinous. But your good mood and optimism are a good compensation!

Job. Career. This month is going to be good though somewhat "motley", when positive influences of the Cosmos will be combined whimsically with negative ones. The former includes normalization of relations with the business partners and, although it may prove to be temporary, it is still better than nothing. Moving step by step, you are strengthening your positions, and your opponents will have to take this into account.

It's possible that some unexpected obstacles will be hampering your work throughout the month, but in the long run, you will overcome them. Your efforts will result in lower uncertainty in the business and it will gradually acquire clarity, shape and structure.

The employee can take a short vacation, and get back to work with renewed vigor, which will result in appreciation and recognition by the boss.

Money. The financial situation is unstable during the whole month. You will have permanent expenses, in one case related to business, and in the other, to the family needs. A ruinous vacation is also quite probable.

Love. Family. Your personal, romantic life will become much more lively. The spouses and the lovers will succeed in improving their relationship, especially if they let their wisdom and undying love help them.

The married people will spend much time with their children, and most of the family budget will be spent for their needs.

For many representatives of your sign, October is a time for parties, entertainment, trips and rest by the warm sea.

The singles can expect an interesting meeting and a bright romance. It's highly probable that the new relationship will bring them to the marriage registration office.

Health. This month, your energy potential is rather high and you will stay healthy.

CANCER

Don't make decisions without listening to all your opponents. Otherwise, you risk breaking your forehead against the walls, which will turn out to be made of armed concrete this time.

Job. Career. The coming weeks will bring you serious battles, in which every attack will cost you a huge effort. The entrepreneurs and managers will face opposition from their steadfast and uncompromising ex-partners. Perhaps, the reason of the conflict will again be large property.

You have faced all this more than once and know how this happens. Most likely, you won't achieve any trade-off this month and the whole thing will be postponed. This looks like a vicious circle, when the situation improves temporarily and then gets worse again, and there is no mutual understanding and agreement.

For the employees, this month is also not very successful. Many will take vacations and focus on their personal business. As to those who keep working, the stars advise not to irritate the boss and do their job diligently.

Money. Your financial situation is just calm. This month won't bring you a big income or a big loss. Towards its end, unexpected expenses are possible, related to the needs of the children and the loved ones.

Love. Family. For many representatives of your sign, the main events will happen at home an inside the family. There is a possibility of a minor renovation, acquisition of things for decorating the home, and other household events, which will make quite restless even the life of the loving spouses.

The quarrelling couples will begin another battle for common property, first of all, for the home other real estate.

In some cases, the children will help improve the situation, but even their efforts will not be enough to reconcile the hostile parents completely.

The lovers will have frequent quarrels, but for them, this month is more or less neutral.

Health. In October, your energy potential is not high, so try not to overestimate your abilities and be moderate.

The elderly and the weak may experience exacerbations of old chronic diseases; in this case, they should avoid self-treatment and consult a good doctor.

LEO

Try not to overestimate your abilities – it won't be easy to solve all the tasks scheduled for this month. But as they say, "slow and steady wins the race."

Job. Career. In October, many representatives of your sign will collaborate actively with their business partners from other cities or countries and do their very best to reach the cherished goal. However, you will face not only successes, but also obstacles. In one case, this can be your technical and documental unpreparedness, in another, some legal problems, in a third - one of the subordinates may be slow or incompetent, which will do harm to the business.

Generally speaking, the entrepreneurs and managers of all levels should pay close attention to their subordinates and, perhaps, think seriously about shuffling the team. This is the right time for those changes!

The employee should respect those who occupy higher positions or are older. This will let you avoid conflicts and make your life easier throughout October. And try to avoid intrigue.

The good news is that you will have more acquaintances and more valuable information, which will eventually give its result.

Money. The financial situation is just calm; this month won't bring any significant success or failures.

Love. Family. Your personal, romantic life is quite OK this month. The lovers and the spouses will travel together, but the stars strongly recommend you to prepare well for it: study the route, and, perhaps, analyze the international situation.

Don't schedule your trip for the first and last days of October because of possible problems on the road.

Relations with the children are quite harmonious. This month, there will be pleasant events in their life, and you can take a very active part in them.

Relations with the relatives can bring a lot of problems, such as claims related to debts or other obligations. In another variant, one of the relatives may fall ill or experience bad times, so your compassion and support will be required.

Health. This month, you are healthy, energetic and enterprising. But the stars strongly recommend you to be cautious when traveling and driving as road accidents are highly probable.

VIRGO

October is very good for making extra money as well as for spending it well. Do everything with pleasure!

Job. Career. In October, your professional activity will be rather high.

The entrepreneurs and the managers will finalize an important project and get a good profit.

Ties with the colleagues from other cities or countries will be very important; there is a chance of business trips, negotiations, phone calls and letters. But not everything will go on smoothly. Annoying incidents are possible in the middle and in the end of October, which will hamper the business. They won't make you change your plans, but you will have to speed up.

Those who are expanding their business will be able to finalize important projects related to real estate.

The employee can get additional assignments and thus make additional money.

Complicated relations with one of the business partners are improving. This will only happen due to your efforts; as to your colleagues, it's possible that they will take no initiative.

Money. Your financial situation is not stable in October. The problem is not lack of money, but the excessive expenses. In one case, it's related to your business, while in the other, to the needs of the family, first of all the children.

Love. Family. In your personal life, what started earlier, will continue in October. First of all, it's continuation or completion of construction, renovation, or other activities aimed at improving your home. Some of you will do it for themselves, others for the children. The latter are the main article of large expenditures in many families. It's now a tradition that the lion's share of the family budget is spent for the children's needs.

Relationships of the lovers can hardly be called good: once again they have to make a choice - love or money? Choose what is more important for you and act accordingly. In another version, the problem is different life outlooks and different value systems. If this is the case, the situation can come to a deadlock...

Many families will have problems with relatives. Some of your family members can't come to terms with each other, and you will have to act as "a dove of peace", which is a difficult task.

Health. In October, your energy potential is not very high, and if your feel that your energy and patience are coming to an end, think about doing yoga, meditating, or walking in a park.

Throughout the month, be careful when traveling and driving.

LIBRA

You will meet your month in full readiness. Yes, you will have to fight again, but every step forward forces the enemy to retreat and brings you closer to victory.

Job. Career. This month, the entrepreneurs and the managers will be restoring order in their business. Once again, the problem will be real estate or other large property. These disputes have been keeping you busy for quite a long time now.

This month, you will use several tools to implement your scenario - from carrots to sticks. This will let you achieve your goal.

Complicated relations with the colleagues from other cities or countries will get better again. But it will be you, not your foreign partners, who will do everything confidently and firmly.

Business trips scheduled for this month will be very successful and help you move your business forward.

The employee's positions will also improve - you will overcome successfully the intrigues of the colleagues and ill-wishers. Many of you will have interesting business trips and an opportunity to present your talents in full splendor.

Money. Your financial situation will also improve, but it won't be quite stable.

Unexpected expenses are possible throughout the month; in one case, they will be related to business, while in the other, to household issues and the children, of course.

You can get decent amounts of money on October 1, 2, 10, 11, 20, 21.

Love. Family. In your personal life, it's still stormy. The quarrelling spouses may begin another round of battles for the property, first o all for the home. This time, you will seize the initiative and even try to run the show. The response to your activity can be very aggressive. You will spend the whole of October fighting.

The loving couples will cooperate to overcome the problems related to their home or other real estate, or to the older family members.

In October, Mars passes into your sign, which means that you will have a lot of energy, and the stars advise you to use it for the sake of peace and mutual understanding.

Health. This month, your energy potential is rather high and you will stay healthy.

SCORPIO

The month is not going to be simple, and it would be better to use it for planning, thus minimizing your activity. In this way, you can structure your thoughts and define your goals.

Job. Career. Throughout the month, the entrepreneurs and the managers should pay much attention to their entourage. You must be ready for possible intrigues of the competitors as well as for appearance of auditors.

Many of you will face resistance of the opponents but will manage to defend their point of view.

Those who have ties with colleagues living in other cities and countries will face problems again. In a general forecast like this, it's hard to say what exactly will happen in each case, but there is a definite reason for concern.

In November, many problems will be resolved, so don't be upset, and act.

Relations with your new business partners are also far from ideal, quarrels erupt periodically, and you will see that not all promises are fulfilled and not all people in your entourage can be trusted.

Money. Despite numerous professional problems, in terms of finance, everything will be OK. The largest amounts can be expected on October 3, 4, 12, 13, 22, 23, 29, 30.

Love. Family. Those whose priority is their personal life, will also face problems.

Throughout the month, be careful with your loved ones and don't trust them unconditionally as it's possible that someone will try to lead you astray.

Many representatives of your sign will have more problems with their relatives. Perhaps the old claims and grievances will be resumed, but in the long run, most of the problems will be resolved - due to your efforts only.

Relationships between the spouses as well as the lovers will become worse. Many will understand that the future is not bright and something has to be done.

All representatives of your sign should take into account that many unpleasant secrets may be revealed in October - both yours and your loved ones'. Be cautious and cover your bases, because now you are quite vulnerable.

Health. Those who have no professional or business difficulties, may have health problems. Aggravation of old diseases or sudden appearance of new ones is possible.

The drivers are advised to be more careful when driving as car accidents and injuries are highly probable throughout this unlucky month.

SAGITTARIUS

In October, you will he great new opportunities. It's time to
get acquainted with them.

Job. Career. In October, your social activity will be very high. Unexpectedly for yourself, you will be very popular and in great demand, and many people will try to help you.

Perhaps you will be supported and patronaged by famous high-position persons. This will let you strike profitable deals and get promoted at your company.

But, as it often happens, luck is not absolute and you can't have the sweet without the sour. This is the case now: some annoying events will hamper the successful course of your business.

The self-employed as well as the managers and employees can face problems inside the team. In one case, some of the team members will act arrogantly and counterpose their interests to the needs of their colleagues, while in another, you will have to improve the new projects, but it will suddenly turn out that the team is not ready for doing it.

Money. This month, you will also have financial difficulties. Your new projects will require investment, and the amount needed may be much higher than expected.

Those whose highest priority is their personal life may spend a lot of money for the needs of the family and children. Expensive purchases are also quite probable, and they will empty the wallets of many representatives of your sign.

Love. Family. You will have a lot of work to do in October and may have no time left for your personal life. Those in love won't see each other as often as they want; the same goes for the spouses.

The stars recommend those who is fond of "sitting between two chairs" to keep their secrets, because this month, those secrets can suddenly be revealed. Many families will have pleasant troubles related to their children, and large expenses for their needs are probable.

Health. In the first and second tenday periods of October, your energy potential is rather high and you will stay healthy.

In the third tenday period, working, communicating and endless bustling will make you feel exhausted. If this is the case, go to a Russian bath, have massage, and relax at your summer house or by a warm sea.

CAPRICORN

No mater what you are going to do this month, it will be a success. You have overcome the organizational barriers, and the final breakthrough is just round the corner.

Job. Career. This month, you will act confidently and energetically, and will definitely achieve success in all your undertakings.

The entrepreneurs will finalize the organizational work and set plans for the future. New promising proposals with great potential are possible, which will mean a new stage in your business. This stage is close, it will take place in 2020.

The employee will negotiate a new job. The negotiations will bring a good result this month or a bit later, and this will be very timely, especially if you have problems with your current job.

At the same time, your character began changing recently: you are now stubborn and uncompromising, often for no reason. All this can affect relations with many people in your entourage.

Don't be too categorical, find compromises, which will make you still more successful!

Money. In October, your financial situation is quite stable, you will be getting money on a regular basis, and its amount will grow.

Estimated dates of getting the largest amounts are October 7, 8, 17, 18, 25, 26.

This month's expenses will not be high, they will be related to your children or partner.

Love. Family. The stars give "green light" to your professional activity, while your personal life will not be perfect.

In the best-case scenario, you simply won't have enough time to spend with your family members and loved ones, which will cause misunderstanding and resentment. Perhaps you just don't have tact and patience to communicate with your loved ones in a better way. Remember about it and be more tactful.

Many families will have problems with their children: the older ones will start a "riot", they want independence and complete freedom; the younger ones won't behave themselves, which is not what you would like to see.

This month is not simple for the lovers: jealousy and resentment are probable. In case of a prolonged quarrel, remember about the above and behave accordingly.

Health. This month, you are quite healthy, just too irritable and proud.

ᗩQUᗩRIUS

In October, you will be trying to go forward as fast as possible, pushing the gas pedal to the limit. But the stars strongly advise you to be very attentive on the road lest you should accidentally run into a deep pit.

Job. Career. This month, you will want to forget about the past and look at the current and future projects from a different angle. But it won't be easy to do as some flaws will make you go back and analyze the unresolved issues.

The entrepreneurs and the managers are recommended to get ready for inspections, quite probable this month. In case of problems, feel free to ask your friends or people having power and authority to help you - their help will be timely and useful.

Relations with the colleagues from other cities or countries are getting much more active, though you will face annoying delays and problems. It's hard to provide details in a general forecast, but there will be a cause for concern.

Get ready for this month's business trips, otherwise they will be less successful than planned.

Money. There won't be any big changes in your financial situation, everything will go on just as before. This month won't bring significant success or big losses.

The estimated dates of getting the largest amounts are October 1, 2, 10, 11, 20, 27, 28.

Love. Family. Your personal life won't be calm. The loving couples will have housing problems: in one case, they will want or have to change their apartment/house, while in the other, they will have to make a renovation or change the interior.

In many families, the atmosphere is changing. You are getting closer to a breakup, which is no one's fault. The reason is a new stage in your life, which means that parting with something and someone is inevitable.

Health. This month, you are healthy, energetic and very enterprising. However, the stars strongly advise you to be more attentive when traveling and driving as road accidents and other problems are quite probable.

pisces

October is a month of team work and intensive communication, sometimes forced. Beware of the "wolves in sheep's clothing" and remember that "all that glitters is not gold."

Job. Career. For you, October is a month of all kinds of organizational events and preparations. Prepare the platform for another breakthrough, which will happen in November or December.

Meanwhile, the stars recommend you to look closely at your entourage as it seems that some of those people are abusing your trust. In one case, those are your old friends, in another, a high-position person. There is a possibility of disputes on financial issues as well as on various debt obligations, both monetary and moral.

Relations with the colleagues from other cities or countries are not smooth. On the way to the goal, you will face unexpected though quite surmountable obstacles.

In fact, your professional affairs are in general on the rise in October, and the problems, if any, will be quite ordinary.

Many representatives of your sign will take a few days off and go away from the fuss and everyday routine. The stars only welcome this decision.

Money. Financially, October can be uneven. And it's not that you won't have enough money, but that you will have more expenses than expected.

In one case, this is related to your business and the need to pay off the old debts, while in the other, to the household problems and your family needs.

Love. Family. In the personal life, you will also have to solve difficult problems related to your friends and loved ones. Not everything is OK in your relations with the friends: in one version, a conflict is possible, in another, someone will need help or advice, especially in financial matters.

There are problems related to your loved ones, too: unexpected quarrels on the smallest issues are possible, when you will have to reconcile the raging relatives.

The stars recommend the lovers to go on vacation together to the warm sea. And even if you have to pay a lot, don't save the money! The trip will help you avoid quarrels, quite likely this month.

Health. In October, your energy potential is not high, so lead a healthy lifestyle and spend the weekends out of town.

NOVEMBER

ARIES

Your dream is just one step away, but it will be very hard to make that step. Cheer up! Every blow delivered by life makes you stronger.

Job. Career. This month, many representatives of your sign will have to "work like a dog" in order to put together the intricate interests of their team members.

Lengthy negotiations on complex financial issues are probable, as well as their slow resolution. It will be possible to achieve a positive result, but this will require much effort, including a lot of paperwork.

Your relations with the colleagues from other cities or countries will improve, and by the end of November, you will reach agreement on some important issues. In the last days of the month, a business trip or arrival of business partners from far away are possible.

Gradually, many representatives of your sign will see new horizons. This is equally true for the employee and for the entrepreneur.

Money. In terms of finance, November is far from easy. The stars advise all representatives of your sign, regardless of their occupation, to be more careful about money as well financial documents. These precautions will let you avoid troubles and losses.

Lengthy negotiations on obtaining a credit and revision of financial obligations are possible, as well as paying old debts off.

Many can count on the support of the business partners or loved ones.

Love. Family. As a rule, many representatives of your sign "take it easy"; in fact, you have nothing to hide! However, this month you will face intrigue, which will spoil your relations with the entourage as well as with your loved one. And if you have common business or financial interests, the situation will become still more complicated.

In the long run, everything will be OK, but in the beginning and in the middle of the month, there will be a reason for concern, so don't raise topics that may have pitfalls, and avoid intrigue. You are not up to such games.

Towards the end of the month, you will be able to go on a trip. Do it! New places and impressions will distract you from numerous problems, which will now look small and irrelevant to you.

Health. This month, your energy potential is not high, so protect your body from the fall colds and lead a healthy lifestyle.

TAURUS

Relations with people are hard to plan. For example, you expect one thing, but get something else. It's exactly what is happening right now.

Job. Career. In November, many representatives of your sign will become dependent on their partners. It's not the most pleasant situation, especially because you will face strange and ambiguous behavior of the people you counted on.

On the other hand, the revolutionary mood, which recently became one of your features, can also hamper normal communication. You want to have everything your way, get out of the usual circle of people and responsibilities and change your life. Right you are! The current stage of your career is coming to an end, and the next year can be exactly like you want.

People you have not seen for a long time can suddenly return to your life. Those can be your old friends and business partners living in other cities or countries, so a proposal to resume collaboration is possible.

You can take the first steps in this direction right away, although the full-scaled work will begin later.

Money. In November, your financial situation is not quite stable. Probably, it will be about loans and credits; negotiations on financial support from stronger partners are probable. Those whose main priority is their personal life can rely on the help from their loved ones.

Love. Family. Your romantic and family life will not be calm. It mostly refers to those born in the period from April 21 to 29. They are in for serious changes in their relationship, which refers to the lovers and the spouses. It's hard to provide details in a general forecast, but the tendency to renew life, as well as the unwillingness to listen and understand can have a very negative impact on your relationship.

On the other hand, your partner may not act in the best way. His/her behavior can be ambiguous, he/she may not be willing to keep their promise, and sometimes will even deceive you. This will be faced by many representatives of your sign.

Relations with the relatives will be a bit better, you can meet with some of them who live in another city or country.

In November, many will be in a nostalgic mood, they will want and be able to meet with their old friends and ex partners, some of them living in another city or country.

Health. This month, your energy potential is not high, but you will not be seriously ill if you take care and are moderate.

Watch your weight! In November and December, you may gain some weight, and losing it will not be easy.

GEMINI

Don't rush to make decisions or hasty promises. Remember that slow and steady wins the race.

Job. Career. Conservatism is not one of your characteristic features, but you will need it in November. Otherwise, you can make mistakes or contact people who will do you harm.

November is good for making a detailed analysis of your business, putting things in order, finding mistakes and making plans to correct them. Mercury, your governor, is moving backwards, which means that the people you met between October 31 and November 20 will subsequently turn out to be quite different than expected and may deteriorate your business.

During this period, you should not make your bright ideas public; keep thinking about them and work on presenting them.

If there are signs of protest and intrigue in the team, don't take anyone's side as you can hardly make an unbiassed assessment of the situation.

At the same time, relations with your regular business partners will improve, you will reach understanding on many issues and outline plans for further work.

Money. Your financial situation will be more or less neutral in November. Perhaps you will negotiate a credit or investments from your business partners, and in late November, you will achieve success.

The largest amounts can be expected on November 6, 7, 16, 17, 24-26.

Love. Family. In your personal life, everything is relatively calm. The spouses and the lovers will spend November in harmony with each other and with family members.

November will only have one peculiarity - many representatives of your sign may be suspicious and jealous, and for no reason. If this is the case, be more careful and try not to aggravate the situation!

Remember that fake news are possible in November, while the rumors and gossip will have nothing to do with real life.

Those sitting between two chairs are recommended to remember that all the secrets will be revealed sooner or later, and this can happen in November.

Health. In November, your energy potential is not high, so get dressed warm and be moderate in everything.

Also, don't fuss and don't be nervous! Being nervous is the cause of all diseases, which is especially true for your sign.

CANCER

Romantic feelings are hard to plan, and this is the case now: you and your partner have quite different opinions. Be careful and try not to make the whole thing worse!

Job. Career. In terms of job and career, this month is not bad.

However, it would be a bad ide to start new projects: in the period from October 31 to November 20, Mercury is moving backwards and this time is better for completing the previously started projects, having old debts paid off, and doing the paperwork. All this will go on smoothly, without delays or problems.

The entrepreneurs and the managers can fully rely on their subordinates, while the employees - on their colleagues. The team is in the middle of a rare period of time when everyone can count on the support of all team members and focus on productive work.

The deteriorated ties with your colleagues from other cities or countries are slowly getting back to normal. There are still problems and the future of these relations is still unclear, but this is better than nothing.

Much work is to be done to normalize the ties, and final success can only be achieved in the spring of 2020. Pave the way to mutual understanding, and everything will be OK!

Money. Your financial situation is stable, money will be coming on a regular basis, and its total amount will increase a little. The estimated dates for receiving the largest amounts are November 8-10, 19, 20, 27, 28.

It is possible that you will have the old debts paid off or find the money you considered lost.

Love. Family. For many representatives of your sign, the most important events of November can happen in their personal lives.

In particular, the spouses will be concerned about their children's future, and in some cases the children will become the main link between the quarreling parents. The same goes for those who have divorced and parted.

Even if full reconciliation is impossible, use this opportunity to communicate normally and resolve peacefully the issues related to your children's future.

The lovers will have a turbulent month. You will experience frequent changes in mood, from joy to disappointment. Your partner may behave in the same way. Stay calm and offer your partner a trip to a place you have already been to. This will stabilize the situation and improve your relationship.

Health. This month, you are quite healthy, though restless and nervous. Your first priority in November is achieving inner balance and harmony. So, watch good movies, meet old friends, and go out of town as often as possible.

LEO

Try not to get overwhelmed with work this month. In fact, this is a month of relaxation.

Job. Career. This month is not very good for your career. The best thing to do would be putting things in order, clarifying relations with your colleagues and subordinates, and doing things that were put off "till better times."

Moving forward is now impossible, but nothing prevents you from preparing the ground for further undertakings. This is especially true for those who plan to take on new, unusual projects or get a new job.

The employees are advised to assess their abilities calmly, abstain from coming up with bold initiatives and, if possible, stay away from the boss. Your positions are vulnerable now, and in case of some misunderstandings, you may consider resignation. If you don't have such plans, be prudent.

It would be a good idea to take a vacation and spend a week or two by the warm sea.

Money. Your financial situation is more or less neutral. There will be no big achievements this month, just as no losses. Both your incomes and expenses are predictable and reasonable.

Love. Family. In November, many representatives of your sign will plunge into the family problems. Minor changes in everyday life are possible – a small renovation, purchase of furniture or other everyday things. Something else is also probable: you will have more guests than usual, and this will make the atmosphere in many families quite restless.

The older children are doing fine, the little ones behave very well.

The lovers' relationship will be improved greatly; an important decision about living together or getting acquainted with the partner's parents is probable.

Family ties still cause a lot of anxiety, the most difficult time in this regard being early November, after which the problem will be somehow solved.

If you have plans for having a rest, the stars advise you to go to a familiar place, otherwise you can easily make a mistake and get disappointed. This advice is only relevant from October 31 to November 20.

Health. This month, your energy potential is not high, frequent states of lethargy and fatigue are possible. The best remedy for this is a full rest and a good sleep.

In the period between November 1 and 7, be careful when traveling or driving a car.

VIRGO

*November is one of busiest months of the year. However,
it is not good for being active - Mercury, your governor,*

is moving backwards, so remember that "slow and steady wins the race."

Job. Career. November will make you do things that may seem boring and not very pleasant. There will be a lot of paperwork and red tape, searching for and registering the documents, as well as talking to numerous bureaucrats. All that will look like a vicious circle - someone is not in the office, some necessary papers are missing, so from time to time you will feel a hamster in a wheel having a very low efficiency coefficient. But cheer up! Towards the end of the month, you will reach the goal, and everything will be OK.

Relations with colleagues from other cities or countries are not stable this month. Your business partners from far away may be very slow fulfilling the obligations, and because of all this, your collaboration may seem unstable and unreliable. But this is not so. Be patient, everything will end up well.

Money. Financially, November is not very good. You will have a big expenditure in early November and, most likely, it will be related to the needs of your family and children.

For various reasons, you will be receiving money later than planned; a decent amount can only be expected towards the end of the month.

Love. Family. Your family life is calm. Using their wisdom and undying love, the loving couples will finish the improvement of the house or other real estate. The disagreements of the past months have been overcome, and now the only concern is the children, whose needs still require considerable amounts of money.

Relations with some of the relatives will be somewhat complicated and, although there is no open confrontation, a cause for concern does exist. It's highly probable that the reason is envy, intrigue and hidden hostility of your relatives. Take this into consideration and behave accordingly.

For the lovers, this month is not good. There is a possibility of misunderstandings, finance-related disagreements, as well as intrigues of the entourage.

You will be able to get out of those problems in late November. Before that, don't listen to rumors and gossip as they can't be trusted.

Health. In November, you are quite healthy and energetic, though restless and fussy. Don't forget about walking in a park or out of town, and going to a sauna together with your good friends.

LIBRA

Don't turn off your path, you are moving in the right direction. And don't be afraid of the obstacles – there is no success without them.

Job. Career. You will dedicate most of November to solving financial problems and will definitely succeed. But wining won't be easy: to reach the goal, you will have to work hard and read a lot of documents.

In early November, a controversial situation is possible. It well be related to real estate, land or other large property. Negotiations will begin, and by the end of the month, the situation will be clarified though not quite normalized yet. It will become clear what obligation each of you has and what should be done to settle the long-standing conflict.

Relations with the colleagues from other cities or countries will improve significantly. Towards the end of the month, successful negotiations and a successful resolution of old problems are possible. Take advantage of this rare opportunity! Business trips scheduled for late November will be very successful.

Money. You will spend most November resolving financial issues and achieve a good result! You will have opportunities to make money, as well as spend it wisely or invest it successfully.

The estimated dates for getting the most substantial amounts are November 7, 8, 16-18, 24, 25.

Large expenses are expected at the very beginning of the month; in one case, they are related to your personal life, while in the other, to business.

Love. Family. There are ongoing problems in your personal life. In the first tenday period of November, the quarrelling and divorcing spouses will have more issues related to real estate. After that, complicated negotiations about resolving the financial claims are possible.

In this difficult period, the relatives will support you, their impact on all family affairs will be absolutely positive.

The loving couples will start renovating their homes. Perhaps they will make large investments in their future city house, apartment or summer house.

Joint trips scheduled for late November will be very successful.

The lovers may have conflicts with their parents or with a senior family member. The probability of this is very high in the period from November 1 to 7, after which the situation will normalize.

Health. This month, your energy potential is not high. If you feel exhausted, the stars recommend you to have a rest for a few days and take care of yourself.

SCORPIO

*The obstacles, quite likely in the first and second tenday
periods of the month, will not stop you. More than that, you
will find the right way to your goal.*

Job. Career. In the first and second tenday periods of November, you will find yourself in various situations - difficult, dangerous, and controversial. Be patient and reasonable, and, if possible, "turn off" your emotions. Some of the problems began last month, such as audits, legal problems, misunderstandings with the business partners who live in another city or country.

You will have to deal with all that practically alone, because this month, no one will help you. Listen to your intuition - it will tell you what to do in any situation.

But, as they say, God only gives us tasks we can solve. It will be true in your case: by the end of the month, you will cope with almost all the problems and even improve your positions.

The last week of the month will bring you the long-awaited victory - both moral and financial. So you are on horseback again!

Money. Your financial situation will improve by the end of the month, but before that, you will have to walk down many roads and turn over tons pf papers.

The largest amount of money will come in the period from November 24 to 28; certain amounts can also be expected on November 8, 9, 19, 20.

Love. Family. Your personal life is restless. Many representatives of your sign can face an unexpected situation, when 'the upper classes have no ability, while the lower classes have no wish.' There will be something your spouse or a permanent partner may disagree with, which should be taken into account in order to avoid aggravation of the situation.

Relations with the children are improving. It is possible that the children will become the main link between the two quarreling spouses.

In the first tenday period of November, the conflict with the closest relatives may continue. But some time later, you will do your best to normalize the situation, and you will succeed.

Health. In November, your energy potential will be much higher, but the stars strongly recommend you to be more careful when traveling or driving. The first week of the month is especially unfavorable in this respect.

SAGITTARIUS

November is a difficult month, and it's better to devote it not to active work but to planning. Sometimes, "sitting in a trench" makes the subsequent "offensive" more successful – like now.

Job. Career. The period from November 1 to 20 can hardly be called successful. All the events scheduled for this period will go slowly and not like expected. Be ready for that!

The entrepreneurs and managers are advised to prepare for inspections that can find out some flaws in your work. There can be misunderstandings inside the team as well as conflicts with some of your employees and subordinates.

All representatives of your sign are advised to be prudent and cautious, and not get into conflicts. You can't expect any fair play now anyway, but intrigue is quite probable.

After November 20, a more favorable period begins, when you can leave the problems behind and continue going up and conquering new mountain tops.

The employee is recommended to do his/her duties diligently, avoiding intrigue and, if possible, not criticizing the boss.

Many representatives of your sign should think about vacation or a few days off.

Money. Financially, November is not good either. You will spend a large amount of money between November1 and 7, and in one case it will be related to business, while in the other, to your children's needs.

The money you expected could come not in full or somewhat late.

You can expect certain amounts on November 1, 2, 11, 12, 20, 21, 29, 30.

Love. Family. In your romantic life, disappointment is possible. At some point, you will feel that your partner has lost interest in you and the relationship is coming to an end. Something else is also possible, namely, you will learn some of your partner's secrets or he/she will learn something about you.

Remember that information you receive in the period from October 31 to November 20 may be unreliable, so don't start jumping into conclusions.

The situation will clear up a little later - in the last days of the month, but for now, be patient and just wait. It will be the best thing you can do under the circumstances.

This advice is equally relevant for the lovers and the spouses.

Health. Those who are lucky not to have professional and personal troubles, may have health problems. Be attentive to your body in the last days of October, the first days of November, as well as in Full

Moon - November 11-13. If necessary, contact an experienced doctor or just take a vacation and devote time to yourself.

CAPRICORN

In November, you will face disorder in your entourage. Cheer up! The problems will end in late November, after which you can relax.

Job. Career. In November, your main concern will be relations with someone of the like-minded people or with high-position persons. There will be delays fulfilling promises given earlier; for some reason, they will be revised.

In early November, serious conflicts are likely, related to the difference in views on the future of the business.

Besides, things important for you can get into a dead end - you will have to find the right people, the necessary documents and, in some cases, it will not be easy.

The situation will change in the third tenday period of the month, when it will become clear that many problems are understandable and can be solved. The stars recommend you to go straight to your goal, and be sure that you will achieve it in the long run.

Relations with the colleagues from other cities or countries are not stable - something is moving, while something is not. But this is a temporary situation - everything will change in December and, of course, for the better.

Money. In November, your financial situation is uneven. There will be many expenses; in one case, they will be related to improving the business, while in the other, to the family needs.

Love. Family. This month, romantic life is like the dim November sky. Relationships become confusing and too complicated. Much will depend on your ability to listen and understand your partner.

When the situation comes to a critical point, you will understand that it's necessary to act. A decisive step is needed, and you will make it. Your partner will react quite favorably.

The spouses are in a more complicated situation; it mainly refers to those who have lost interest in each other. There may be conflicts related to everyday problems, as well as to the children's future.

The loving couples are mostly concerned with their children. The young ones' behavior is quite unpredictable, a "riot" is possible. You definitely know better, but maybe you should give your children a little independence and freedom?

If money is involved, decide for yourself how much you can spend, and what for. And most importantly, will the decision be correct? A lot depends on how you answer these questions, so take your time and think well.

Health. In November, you are energetic and quite healthy, but the stars strongly advise you not to work too much - Saturn in your sign wants careful attitude to the body and a healthy lifestyle.

AQUARIUS

The possible obstacles that you are going to face this month will not stop you. More than that, they may stimulate progress. In the meantime, be patient and act slowly.

Job. Career. You are now focused on your job and career.

The entrepreneurs and the managers will finalize the projects they launched earlier, working together with the most reliable employees.

In the period from October 31 to November 20, Mercury is moving backwards, so many of your undertakings will be hampered for various reasons. The competent people may be absent; besides, you will have to find and edit some boring documents. This can be somewhat annoying, but you will be able to look at your work from another angle, find the mistakes and correct them.

Your friends or some high-position persons will make the difference this month. Their influence on all the month's events will be absolutely positive. This will be especially obvious in the second half of November.

Changes are underway at the employee's company, though not painful for him/her. After the difficult period from October 31 to November 20, many representatives of your sign will even improve their positions.

In the first tenday period of November, relations with the colleagues from other cities or countries will become complicated again. But the subsequent negotiations and meetings will gradually resolve all the issues.

Money. In November, your financial situation is stable. Possible changes at work will not deteriorate this situation, the money will keep coming on a regular basis and in quite predictable amounts.

The estimated dates of getting the most substantial amounts are November 5-7, 15-17, 24, 25.

There will be few expenses this month, all of them will be predictable and reasonable.

Love. Family. In November, your personal life can go to the background as the main thing for you now is your job. However, the married people should not relax as rather complex processes are going on in your entourage, which require your close attention. Cooling has begun quietly and almost imperceptibly in your relationship.

This is a lengthy though very important process that manifests a new stage in your life. Everything will change in a couple of years, but presently, the stars are gradually preparing you for the future changes. In another version, the relationship itself will change, and this will happen without suffering and separation.

Many have plans related to housing, but those plans will become reality in 2020.

Health. In November, your energy potential is high enough and you will stay healthy.

pisces

For you, November is a very "changing" month. There will be a lot of opportunities, which will require preparation and additional effort.

Job. Career. This month, many representatives of your sign will open up a window into a bright future. It's quite realistic, but there are many obstacles to overcome on the road to success.

In particular, the entrepreneurs and the managers are going to have lengthy talks about the new, promising projects. It's OK, but from October 31 to November 20, there is a possibility of red tape, lack of the right people, and other problems hampering the business.

Those who have connections with their colleagues from other cities or countries will also face difficulties: the faraway partners can behave inconsistently, and their actions will delay important decisions on the promising and long-awaited projects.

But in the third tenday period of November, all obstacles will be overcome, and you will have the cherished 'scarlet flower' in your hands.

During this period, the employee can be promoted or get a job offer.

Business trips scheduled for the period from October 31 to November 20 may not work well, that's why they should be prepared carefully.

Money. In terms of finance, November is more or less neutral. There is no big income this month, but you hope to have it. Your expectations will definitely come true in the nearest future. This month, you can count on certain amounts on November 8, 9, 24-28. Most of the expenses will be made during the first week of the month.

Love. Family. In the personal, romantic life, nostalgic moods will prevail. After another conflict, quite likely in early November, both parties will try to normalize the situation. It's hardly possible to say what exactly they will do, but towards the end of the month, peace will be restored.

However, many representatives of this sign will see people from the past on their horizon. Those are old friends and ex partners; in some cases, they will come from other cities or countries.

Health. In November, your energy potential is rather high, and you will stay healthy.

However, in the first tenday period of the month, the stars strongly recommend you to be cautious when traveling and driving.

DECEMBER

ARIES

The last month of the year will be dynamic and very successful. It seems that you have grabbed the Bird of Luck by the tail!

Job. Career. In December, your professional activity will be rather high. You are raising step by step to a higher level, and this will continue for at least 3 years. Besides the projects you have already launched, you will have new proposals having good perspectives. Relations with the colleagues from other cities or countries still require your special attention. However, the situation looks clearer and thus more solvable.

Your remote business partners have to take your position into account, or they simply understand that collaboration is better and more beneficial than confrontation.

The employees can expect a professional and financial breakthrough at the current company or an unexpected and lucrative offer from a large, promising one.

Trips scheduled for December will be successful, but you should remove the period from December 8 to 10 from your schedule.

Money. Your financial situation will improve, the money will be coming on a regular basis and, surprisingly, it will be much more than you expected. The dates of getting the largest amounts are December 8-10,

17, 18, 26, 27. You won't have many expenses, and all of them will be predictable and reasonable.

Love. Family. This month, you will be so busy at work that you will have to forget about your personal life. To avoid misunderstandings and conflicts, the stars recommend you to explain the situation to your loved ones; there is a chance that they will understand you. More than that, in some cases, they will help you morally, and, if necessary, financially.

It's possible that you will go on shirt trips together, which always strengthen marital unions and is equally good for those in love.

Health. This month, you are healthy and energetic, and will impress everyone greatly.

TAURUS

December marks the end of an important stage in your business as well as in your personal life. You will have a lot of new opportunities, and your life will change.

Job. Career. December is an important month for finalizing the long-term real-estate related projects, as well as for solving many organizational problems.

Your contacts with the colleagues from other cities or countries will become more active. It is possible that former collaboration will be resumed, though on a different, more up-to-date basis.

Many of you will have plans for moving and setting up a business in another city or country. The first steps in this direction will be made this month. Many controversial issues that have been bothering you throughout the year will be resolved in December or a little later.

Business trips scheduled for this month, especially for late December, can be very successful.

Money. In terms of finance, December is not very good. You will have a lot of expenses related to your business or to your personal life. Many will pay off the long-standing loan.

Love. Family. In your personal life, positive processes are going on. This month, you will finalize the renovation or move.

In some cases, you will change not only your home, but the city or country of residence. Your friends or faraway relatives will help you.

Old relationships will be resumed. It's possible that your ex-partner will return to your life, and all your life changes will have something to do with that.

Trips scheduled for late December or for January 2020 will be very successful.

Health. In December, your energy potential is not high, but you won't have anything serious if you lead a healthy lifestyle and take care of yourself in the best way possible. In this respect, the hardest days may be the Full Moon days - December 11, 12.

GEMINI

December is a busy though rather fruitful month. Many events can be beneficial for you provided that you come to terms with your entourage.

Job. Career. Throughout December, most representatives of your sign will be clarifying their business partnership relations.

The entrepreneurs and the managers will have a strong support, both moral and financial. This will strengthen your professional positions and have a very good impact on your business.

However, the stars recommend you to be careful when signing documents on collaboration: it is possible that taking help, you can get dependent on those who give it to you.

On the other hand, your plans are only possible if you collaborate with stronger and more influential partners. So you should look for the golden mean and always be on alert.

The employee's work is going on well, but you should understand that part of your work is coming to an end. Change is possible in a year, that is rather soon.

Money. This month, all your financial affairs can move forward due to your business partners' financial support. You can get a credit on very good terms, as well as loans or even an unexpected inheritance.

Those who have nothing to do with business can count on the support of their loved one whose business is on the rise.

Love. Family. Important changes are also possible in your personal life. The singles can make a fateful decision about marriage or cohabitation and will think of a new home. This will go on in different periods of the next year, but some important steps can be taken as early as December 2019.

Besides the newlyweds, many representatives of your sign will think of having a new home and thus exchanging or purchasing an apartment or a city or country house, and find the required amount of money.

Health. This month, your energy potential is not high. Besides, the large volume of work and various family responsibilities will make you feel not very confident and cheerful by the end of the month. In this case, take care of your body and its natural needs - rest and sleep.

CANCER

There are things that separate people, but there are those that unite them. The latter will be much more numerous in December!

Job. Career. December is the month of completing some of your projects and analyzing the situation. You did very well in 2019, and now it's the best time for making plans for the future. Old ties will be renewed, people from your past will appear on the horizon – your former business partners and old friends. You can also have new powerful friends. All these relations will make up the next year's background and have a positive impact on your business.

Relations with colleagues from other cities or countries will be somewhat better, and this positive process will continue in the future.

Hostility with one of your opponents will disappear gradually - due to the ultimate breakup or, on the contrary, improvement in your relations.

The employee's positions will become somewhat better, he/she will have new patrons, who will provide their protégé with very important support.

Money. In terms of finance, December is just calm. There won't be big achievements or losses. The estimated dates of receiving the highest amounts are December 6, 7, 15, 16, 24, 25.

Love. Family. There are many changes in your personal life, mostly pleasant ones.

The singles can meet new interesting people, and those relations will definitely continue in the future. Most likely, this is your destiny. In one case, those are people from your past, in the other – someone older than you, very influential and having serious connections.

The quarreling spouses will restore their relationship. In one case, the children will make the difference, while in the other, both spouses will understand that "a bad peace is better than a good fight." The more so that the peace doesn't have to be bad at all. It can be full and unconditional.

Health. This month, your energy potential is not high. Too many responsibilities and meetings may not only make your life brighter, but also exhaust you. So use the weekends for rest, and remember about the benefits of a full sleep.

LEO

December is one of the most interesting months of the year. Both personal and business-related changes are possible. And those are changes for the better!

Job. Career. December gives many representatives of your sign excellent opportunities to show their talents in their full splendor. The entrepreneur and the manager will get a new, very promising and profitable project, which will become their main source of income for years to come.

The employee can get a promotion, or his/her talents will be in demand at another company. In either case, it's a win-win situation, although the work will be difficult and require a lot of time and effort.

Money. Your financial situation will also improve. Money will be coming on a regular basis, and its amount will increase significantly.

The estimated dates of getting the biggest amounts are December 8, 9, 17, 18, 26, 27.

This month's expenses will be related to the children, as well as to the coming holiday.

Love. Family. In your personal life, everything is calm. The married people will put their home in order getting ready for the year's most cheerful holiday. The children mostly make you feel happy. Their life's silver lining will continue, it's reason being, in particular, the parents' efforts.

For the lovers, this month is also not bad. They will plan a trip and go somewhere in late December or next January.

This month, many representatives of your sign will visit all kinds of parties and other entertainment events.

Health. In December, you are healthy, energetic and very attractive, and everyone will notice that.

VIRGO

The personal project, which required so much effort, comes to a logical end. You are approaching a new chapter of your life.

Job. Career. In December, the entrepreneur and the manager will put things in order and finalize an important project related to arranging premises, construction, or other real-estate-related business. This time, all such undertakings will go on calmly, without delays.

Conflicts with some of your business partners are no longer important as you have all necessary facts and documents to influence them.

Business relations with the partners from other cities or countries are going on rather well, there are no more disagreements, and although this is a temporary situation, "a bad peace is better than a good fight."

The employee will probably think about having a new job and take the first steps in this direction. He/she can get interesting offers from the faraway colleagues, and plan moving.

Money. In terms of finance, December can be uneven. There will be a lot of expenses, so towards the end of the year, your wallet will be empty. But the good news is that the money will be spent for a reason, and the December spending will be pleasant and reasonable.

Love. Family. Many representatives of your sign will devote most of December to their loved ones. Renovation is coming to an end, both in your home and in the children's.

Relationships with the children are getting better, and this will continue in the future. Family ties are also improving, and if a serious conflict among the closest relatives was looming in the recent past, now it's time to stop and put up.

Your relations with the partner, which were somewhat spoiled by various domestic problems, will become softer, although each party will remain unconvinced.

Health. In December, you are quite healthy and work diligently. However, there is a weight gain tendency, so exercise and try not to eat too much.

LIBRA

Whatever you do is a success. You are having more supporters and fewer opponents.

Job. Career. This is going to be a bright and very successful month. You will have business trips, negotiations, meetings, and successful agreements. The most probable topic of discussions will again be real estate and land, and this time, you will definitely win. As to improving what you get as a result the victory, it will be carried out successfully in 2020.

At the same time, the stars keep advising you to be more attentive to your subordinates, who are still clumsy and incompetent and just hamper the business. It's not excluded that you will once again face deception and unscrupulousness of those whose direct duty is to support and help you.

The employee can consider starting a family business. At the same time, he/she has a great opportunity not to quit his/her job and, as they say, "sit between two chairs", though successfully.

Money. Your financial positions are stable, and there is an obvious positive tendency. The money will be coming on a regular basis, its amount will increase significantly. The estimated dates of getting the most substantial amounts are December 3, 4, 13, 14, 22, 23 as well as 31. Real-estate operations can also bring you some money. Expenses are few as well as predictable and reasonable.

Love. Family. This month, your personal life is as important for you as your career. Various real estate operations are possible, such as exchanging your apartment/house, its acquisition or sale. In some cases, the last month of the year will manifest the beginning to this process, while the remaining issues will have to be put off till 2020.

The loving spouses will solve their problems, as well as those who decided to separate.

Relations with relatives go on in the right direction. Some misunderstandings, quite likely in the middle of the month, won't affect the atmosphere of trust and friendship.

The lovers will decide on cohabitation, and their parents will help them a lot.

Health. In December, you are healthy, energetic and charming, which everyone will notice.

SCORPIO

*You keep moving forward. There are many opportunities,
and you should get to know them better!*

Job. Career. There will be a change this month. The entrepreneurs and the managers will decide on improving the ties with the colleagues from other cities or countries, and maybe starting a business in a faraway place. In this case, your relatives and friends will help you.

Besides, you will have new people in your entourage, who will also help you in your business.

The employee can get a job offer from a larger company and his/her job will imply business trips. In another variant, his/her talents will be appreciated at the current company and he/she will be offered another, more interesting position.

The relatives will make a positive impact on your career, and in some cases, you may be involved in a business related to the older relatives.

Money. Your financial affairs are on the rise; the estimated dates of getting the most substantial amounts of money are December 6, 7, 15, 16, 24, 25. In December, your expenses are mainly related to the children or the needs of the close relatives.

Love. Family. Your personal life is calm. After the storms of the recent past, the families will resume living peacefully. Both partners will understand that they are moving in the same direction and aiming at the same target. Steam was blown off, you know about your mutual affection and, if necessary, will always help each other.

You may plan relocation. Trips scheduled for December will be very successful.

The singles and those disappointed in their previous affections may contact the ex-partner living in another city or country. The result can't be detailed in a general forecast, but there is a chance of continuation.

The influence of the relatives on your affairs, both personal and professional, is quite significant and quite positive.

Health. In December, you are healthy, energetic, and lucky. All diseases will hold off.

SAGITTARIUS

In December, you can make a giant leap into the future. Every day brings new opportunities to you, so hurry to use them!

Job. Career. The last month's problems are left behind, all misunderstandings are being resolved successfully, and you are opening the door to a better future!

This month, you will have an offer which, as they say, can't be rejected. This is a new and maybe unusual project, which will bring you both professional success and good money.

The employee will be promoted or, somewhat unexpectedly, offered a new position with good financial perspectives. That's definitely a win-win situation.

Money. Your financial positions will be getting better. The largest amount can be expected in mid December; certain amounts can be received on December 8-10, 17, 18, 26, 27.

Many representatives of your sign will rise to a higher financial level, which, after the difficulties of the recent past, will be very important.

Love. Family. In your personal life, everything is OK. Both the lovers and the spouses will spend December peacefully and calmly.

Important real-estate operations are planned, but those are just plans so far; you will take active steps in this direction in 2020.

Many representatives of your sign will celebrate the Christmas at home, with their loved ones.

Health. This month, your energy potential is rather high, but a difficult time is ahead, when you will have to be more attentive to your body and take care of yourself in every possible way.

CAPRICORN

Jupiter moves into the sign of Capricorn, which means that you are going to have lots of excellent opportunities. And in 2020, your talents will unfold in full splendor!

Job. Career. In December, there will be two different trends for many representatives of your sign. One is finalizing complex organizational projects that have taken more than a year. The other is the appearance of new plans and promising projects. You have dreamed about all that for so long, and now it's time to know what's in store for you.

Your old friends or people who occupy a high social position can help you in your business, and their help will be quite beneficial for you.

Relations with your colleagues from other cities or countries are becoming more predictable; there will be a tendency towards much better relations, which will continue in 2020.

A new chapter will also open in the employee's life. If you want to get a new job, this is the best time for doing that. Negotiate, communicate with your friends, and everything will be OK! The luckiest can get what they want right now, in December, while others - in January or February 2020.

Money. Your financial situation is calm, the expenses are moderate, the incomes are stable. However, in the middle of the month, a pleasant surprise is possible, such as a gift or a lottery prize. Try your luck, and you can win!

Love. Family. The stars will not leave your personal life without attention. The singles as well as those disappointed in their previous attachments can have an unbelievable romance, with an interesting development and unpredictable finale. Is the game worth the candle? It surely is!

The loving spouses can have unexpected addition to the family, such as new children or grandchildren, or the corresponding plans.

Relations with the older children, whose business is on the rise, will improve.

Thanks to your efforts, complicated relations with a family member will normalize gradually, and you will begin communicating in a normal way.

Health. This month, you are energetic, healthy and completely focused on a better future.

AQUARIUS

In the near future you will see that the project that required a lot of your time and effort is coming to an end. But you won't have time to relax - a new chapter is opening in your life.

Job. Career. The outgoing year hasn't been bad for you. You have done a lot, but a different time is coming - calmer, more stable and predictable.

The managers and entrepreneurs will expand their business, many will be engaged in construction and numerous organizational events. And in this respect, December is a transitional month.

The employee will also be busy strengthening his/her positions and covering his/her bases. Those who were promoted in 2018, should get ready for conquering new heights in 2019, which will happen at the end of next year or in 2021.

In 2020, constructors and those who work with real estate will be especially successful, and in December, the first steps will be taken in that direction.

Money. Your financial situation is stable. Besides the regular income, many can make additional money through successful real-estate operations. You can get a good credit, support from your business partners, or help from your loved ones. An unexpected inheritance or financial support from the parents are also probable.

Love. Family. Changes in your personal life are also possible. Many representatives of your sign will decide to move, purchase a new home or renovate the old one completely.

There are other options, for example, addition to the family, such as new children and grandchildren, or the corresponding plans.

The lovers will decide to get married or live together, and their parents or family members will help them.

Health. In December, you are healthy, energetic and completely focused on the bright future.

pisces

You succeed in everything you do, you are popular, everyone wants to be closer to you. It seems that you have reached your goal.

Job. Career. In December, your activeness is at its peak. You can advance your old projects and have unexpected opportunities.

You will meet powerful and influential people, who will offer you what you have been dreaming about. In some cases, important proposals will come from the partners living in other cities or countries. Business trips and immediate signing of new contracts are possible.

It's not excluded that your old friends or well-known high-position and wealthy people will take part in your business and you will benefit from that greatly.

The employee can reach another step on the social success ladder, such as a promotion at his/her current company or a new, more interesting and prestigious job. The stars are providing powerful support to you, and all you need to do is to act brightly, boldly, and freshly.

Money. Taking into account the state of the arts in your business, you will have no financial problems. Money will be coming on a regular basis and in large amounts. This positive process will continue in 2020.

Love. Family. There are 2 different tendencies in your personal life. Those disappointed in their previous affections and the singles can count on the renewal of an old relationship; one can even say that the old love will suddenly flare up again.

In another case, an unexpected trip and the appearance of a new person will also make your heart beat harder... In a word, there are many opportunities. You don't have to make use of each one, but it's great that they do exist.

Many will have better relations with the relatives and meet with those of them who live in another city or country.

Health. Throughout December, you are energetic, healthy, and very popular.

We and Our Zodiacal Connections (Compatibility of Zodiac Signs)

Often, when communicating with people at various levels, we feel that someone brings us something good, and we take a liking to him or her, while another person makes us feel hostility, distrust and fear. People say for a reason that "the first impression is the most correct one." Can this be explained in terms of astrology? Are there people who initially bring us trouble and unhappiness, and how can we detect them?

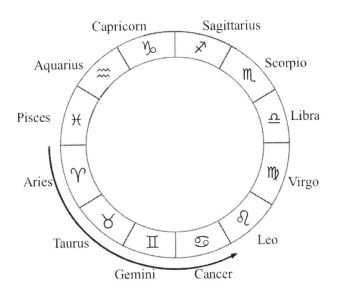

Without going into the astrological subtleties not clear to an unprepared reader, it is possible to name the attributes according to which all kinds of relations will develop, both in business and in private life. Let's start with problematic unions. The most difficult relations are with our **8th sign**. For example, for Aries it is Scorpio, for Taurus - Sagittarius, etc. To find your 8th sign, you need to look at the eighth sign on the Zodiac circle moving counter-clockwise, assuming your own sign to be the first one (see the Figure above). This is also how other signs are to be found.

Ancient astrologers called the 8th sign the symbol of death, destruction, fatal love, and bizarre attachments. This pair is called in astrology "slave-master" or "rabbit and boa constrictor", the role of the "master" and "boa constrictor" being played by our 8th sign.

This union is especially difficult for politicians and business people.

Here is an example of recent political confrontation in the USA: Donald Trump is a Gemini, while Hilary Clinton is a Scorpio. Gemini is the 8th sign for Scorpio, and, despite the fact that many were sure that Clinton would be elected President, she lost.

Here are some historical examples. Hitler was a Taurus, and his opponents were two Sagittarius - Stalin and Churchill. The end of their confrontation is well known. Another interesting fact is that Russian Victory Marshals, Konstantin Rokossovsky and Georgy Zhukov, were also born under the sign of Sagittarius; they dealt crushing blows to Hitler's army and became the symbol of the end of the Third Reich.

Lenin was also a Taurus; his comrade-in-arms, Stalin, took away all Lenin's powers in the latter's last years of life, perhaps caused Lenin's death and subsequently destroyed Lenin's entire entourage. Stalin (Sagittarius) was the 8th sign for Lenin.

Business ties with our 8th sign are also dangerous, they ultimately bring us stresses and losses, both financial and moral. So, don't mess with your 8th character and never fight it - your chances to win are extremely small!

Such relationships are very interesting in terms of love. We are drawn to our 8th sign as by a magnet, because in terms of sex, this union may be the best, but for a family life, it is very difficult. "Feeling bad while being together, feeling worse while being apart."

Take the world-famous lovers as an example - George Sand (Cancer) and Alfred de Musset (Sagittarius). For Sagittarius, Cancer is the 8th sign, and the story of their crazy two-year love was the subject of attention across France. Critics and writers were divided into "Mussulists" and "Sandists", they debated fiercely about who was to blame for the sad ending of the love story - he or she. How much energy had to be spent to excite the minds of humankind for so long? However, that energy was destructive for the famous couple. In their hearts, passions raged, but both of them were just not able to understand what was going on.

Georges Sand wrote to Musset, "I don't love you anymore, and I will always adore you. I don't want you anymore, and I can't do without you. It seems that nothing but a heavenly lightning can heal me by destroying me. Good bye! Stay or go, but don't tell me that I am not suffering. This is the only thing that can make me suffer even more, my love, my life, my blood! Go away, but kill me, leaving." Musset said a short phrase, but its magical power surpasses George Sand's tirade, "When you embraced me, I felt something that is still bothering me, making it impossible for me to approach another woman." These two people loved each other passionately and lived together for two years as on a powder keg, their life being full of passions, hatred and treachery.

When someone unites with their 8th sign, there won't be any peace; for those who love borderline, dramatic situations in Dostoevsky's style, these alliances are very attractive. The first to cool down is, as a rule, our 8th sign.

If, by the will of fate, our child is born under the 8th sign, he or she will be very different from us and, in some ways, not up to our expectations. At best, he or she will choose their own way.

For business and political relations, the union with the 12th sign is also complicated.

For example, Trump is a Gemini, while Angela Merkel is a Cancer. Trump is the 12th sign for Merkel, that's why their relations are strained and complicated. We can assume that the American president will achieve his political goals, while Merkel will lose in the confrontation.

Such were the relations of Mikhail Gorbachev (Pisces) and Boris Yeltsin (Aquarius). For Gorbachev, Yeltsin was the 12th sign, who managed to debunk the Perestroika hero.

Even ancient astrologers noticed that the relations with one's 12th sign cannot develop evenly, it is one of the most bizarre and problematic alliances. They are our secret enemies, who can ingratiate themselves with us and know our innermost secrets. Contacting them, we get confused and make mistakes; they seem to be digging a pit for us. Among the Roman emperors murdered by their entourage, there was an interesting regularity – each murderer represented the 12th sign of the murdered one.

In Russian history, we also see the pernicious chain: the German princess Alexandra (Gemini) married the last Russian esar Nicholas II (Taurus) - he was her 12th sign and brought her a tragic death. The evil genius of this family, Grigory Rasputin (Cancer), who made friends with Tsarina Alexandra, his 12th sign, was killed as a result of that unusual friendship. As you can see, it was also a group of people very attached to each other, but mutually destroying each other. Pyotr Stolypin, who intended to take Russia to a higher economic and social level, was an Aries, i.e. the 12th sign of Nicholas II; he made all the tsar's weakness obvious, and the tsar's authority fell after Stolypin's death.

So it makes sense to look attentively at your 12th sign, especially if you have business ties. Usually, these people know much more about us than we want them to, and, if necessary, they reveal our secrets. However, the beginning of these connections is, as a rule, not bad. Sometimes, the two people are friends, but one of them can later betray the other one or blow a secret inadvertently.

In terms of love relationships, our 12th sign is softer, he/she can take care of us and surround us with tender affection. He/she knows and understands our weaknesses. But it is he/she who guides us, although it is sometimes almost imperceptible. Mutual sexual attraction is usually strong.

For example, Megan Clark is a Leo, the 12th sign for Prince Harry, who is a Virgo. Despite the fact that Queen Elizabeth II was against the misalliance, Harry's love was so strong that they did get married.

If the 12th sign is our child, it becomes clear some time later that he/she knows all our secrets, even those he/she is not supposed to know. It is very difficult to control such children as they will do everything their own way.

Relations with our 7th **sign** are also interesting. They are our opposite, learning something new from us, while we have something to learn from them. This union, in business and personal relations, can be very good and interesting provided that both partners are quite intelligent and have high moral standards. At a lower level, this means constant misunderstandings and rivalry. Marriage or cooperation with the 7th sign can only exist as a union of two full-fledged individuals, in which case love, significant business achievements and social success are possible.

However, the unions of such partners can be not only interesting, but also quite complicated.

An example - Angelina Jolly, a Gemini, and Brad Pitt, a Sagittarius. This is a typical alliance with the 7th sign - it's bright, interesting, but quite stressful. This couple can quarrel and part from time to time, but they never lose interest in each other.

It may be for this reason that these ties are more stable at a mature age, when people understand of the true essence of marriage and partnership. For large-scale political relations, this is a state of cold war and eternal tension, for example, Yeltsin (Aquarius) and Bill Clinton (Leo).

Relations with our **9th sign** are very good, he/she is our teacher and advisor, who can reveal to us something that we don't know yet. Very often, relations with him/her result in traveling or relocating. The union can be beneficial in terms of business and contribute to spiritual growth.

An example: although Trump and Vladimir Putin are political opponents, they can come to terms and even feel a certain affection to each other. Putin is a Libra, while Trump is a Gemini, the 9th sign for Putin.

This union is quite harmonious for conjugal and love relationships.

We treat our **3rd sign** somewhat condescendingly. They are like our younger siblings, we can teach them, and they will listen attentively. More often than not, our younger brothers and sisters are born under this sign. In terms of personal relationships and sex, the union is not very interesting and can end quickly (although different options are possible). In terms of business, it is not bad as it often connects partners from different cities or countries.

We treat our **5th sign** as a child. The circumstances are such that we must take care of him/her. The union is not very good for business, since our 5th sign wins in terms of finance and useful connections, giving us little in return, except for love or sympathy. But he/she is very good for family and love relationships, especially if the 5th sign is a woman. If a child is born under this sign, relations with his/her parents are smooth, love and understanding on both sides will last a lifetime.

The **10th sign** is a born boss. Here everything depends on the spiritual level of the people. Both good and tense relations are possible. They are often mutually beneficial in good periods as well as mutually disruptive in bad ones. In family relations, our 10th sign always tries to be the leader and does it depending on his/her intelligence and upbringing.

Our **4th sign** protects our home and can act as a sponsor, which strengthens our positions, either financial or moral. But in all cases, his/her advice should be heeded, it can be very efficient, albeit quite unobtrusive. If a woman acts in this role, family relations can be long and romantic, since all the spouse's wishes are usually met, one way or another. Sometimes, such couples achieve great social success (Hilary Clinton - Scorpio and Bill Clinton - Leo). If the husband is the 4th sign for his wife, he is a henpecked man. There is often a strong sexual attraction in this case. Our 4th sign can improve our living conditions and take care of us in a fatherly way. If a child is born under this sign, he/she can live next to us and patronize us tenderly.

We are often tied with our **11th sign** by friendly or patronizing relations; we treat him/her with reverence, while they treat us with friendly condescension. Sometimes, these relations develop in the "older brother" or "high-ranking friend" style. Indeed, older brothers and sisters are often born under this sign. In terms of personal relationships and sex, the 11th sign is always inclined to enslave us. This tendency is most clearly manifested in such alliances as Capricorn - Pisces, Leo - Libra. A child born under this sign achieves greater success than his parents, they can be proud of him/her.

Our **2nd sign** should bring us money or some other benefits, we have a lot from him/her both in business and in family life. In married couples, the 2nd sign usually protects money for the benefit of the family. He is very attached to us in a sexual way.

Our **6th sign** is our 'slave', we always benefit from working with him/her, and it's very difficult for him/her to get out of our influence. In the event of enmity, he/she receives a powerful retaliatory strike, especially if he/she provokes the conflict. In personal relations, we can somehow destroy them, making them dance to our tune. For example, a husband doesn't allow his wife to work, or family circumstances develop in such a way that she gradually becomes lost as an individual, although she is surrounded by care. This is the best-case scenario, worse options are possible. Our 6th sign has a strong sexual affection for us, because for him/her, we are the fatal 8th sign. We are, too, but we cool down quickly and often make all kinds of claims. If the relations with our 6th sign are long, there is a danger of routine, boredom and stagnation, which ultimately destroys the relationship. A child born under the 6th sign needs a particularly careful attitude, he/she can feel fear or embarrassment communicating with us, his health often needs increased attention. We must also remember that he/she is very different from us emotionally.

And, finally, relations with **our own sign**. Scorpio-Scorpio and Cancer-Cancer get along well; it is hard to say anything specific about the rest, but in most cases, our own sign is of little interest to us as it carries similar energy. Sometimes, relations develop as rivalry, both in business and in love.

There is another interesting detail: We are often attracted to two representatives of the same sign. For example, a man's wife and mistress have the same sign. As a result of the confrontation, the stronger character displaces the weaker one. Here is an example: Prince Charles is a Scorpio, while Princess Diana and Camilla Parker Bowles were both born under the sign of Cancer. Camilla was more grabby and won in that confrontation.

Of course, in order to draw definitive conclusions, we need an individual horoscope, but the above trends will, one way or another, manifest themselves.

Tatiana Borsch

Made in the USA
Columbia, SC
24 November 2018